The Glory of
TITLETOWN

The Glory of

TITLETOWN

THE CLASSIC
GREEN BAY PACKERS PHOTOGRAPHY
OF VERNON J. BIEVER

VERNON BIEVER
PETER STRUPP, EDITOR

TAYLOR PUBLISHING · DALLAS, TEXAS

Some quotations in this book were reported in the *The New York Times, Chicago Tribune, Boston Globe, USA Today, Milwaukee Journal-Sentinel, Time,* and the Associated Press.

Copyright © 1997 by Taylor Publishing Company
Text copyright © 1997 by Peter Strupp and Taylor Publishing Company
All photographs © Vernon J. Biever

Published by Taylor Publishing Company
1550 West Mockingbird Lane
Dallas, Texas 75235

Book design by Mark McGarry
Set in Minion & Huxley Vertical

Library of Congress Cataloging-in-Publication Data
Biever, Vernon J.
  The glory of Titletown : the classic Green Bay Packers photography of Vernon J. Biever /
Vernon Biever, Peter Strupp; foreword by Bart Starr
         p. cm.
   ISBN 0−87833−990−6
   1. Green Bay Packers (Football team)—History—Pictorial works. I. Strupp, Peter. II. Title.
GV956.G7B54 1997
796.332'64'0977563—dc21   97−20810
                                                                            CIP

Printed in the United States of America
10 9 8 7 6 5 4 3 2 1

To my wife, Frances, for her unselfish support and patience, and for keeping many meals warm until after the game. To my children, Barbara, John, and Jim, whose encouragement throughout my career contributed to the success I have enjoyed. And to the many friendships that were fostered while photographing the world's greatest football team, the Green Bay Packers.

V.J.B.

To Vince Lombardi for then; to Mike Holmgren, Ron Wolf, and Bob Harlen for now; and to my brother, Tobin Strupp, the first great fan with whom I shared the game.

P.S.

ACKNOWLEDGMENTS

Grateful thanks are extended to the following active members and alumni of the Green Bay Packers and members of the sports media for their generous participation in this project: Donnie Anderson; Edgar Bennett; Ken Bowman; John Brockington; Robert Brooks; Tony Canadeo; Mark Chmura; Paul Coffman; Willie Davis; Lynn Dickey; Boyd Dowler; Brett Favre; Marv Fleming; Craig Hentrich; Mike Holmgren; Paul Hornung; Scott Hunter; Chris Jacke; Gary Knafelc; Jerry Kramer; James Lofton; Chester Marcol; Mike McCoy; Max McGee; Mark Murphy; Ray Nitschke; Brian Noble; Lee Remmel; Dave Robinson; Bart Starr; Jim Taylor; George Teague; Fuzzy Thurston; Reggie White; Willie Wood; John Biever, *Sports Illustrated*; Jim Irwin, WTMJ; Steve Sabol, NFL Films; and George Vecsey, *The New York Times*.

PREFACE

I certainly didn't discover Vernon Biever. By the time I was born he was already one of the most accomplished sports photographers working, associated with the Green Bay Packers for twenty years. By the time I was out of grade school, his work was hanging in the National Portrait Gallery in Washington. By the time I graduated from high school, his work was in the Hall of Fame in Canton. But in a personal way, I feel that I made a rediscovery.

To grow up in Wisconsin is to grow up with the Packers. It's kind of a blessing for a child. The world happened in New York and Los Angeles and Washington, D.C., but we had the Green Bay Packers. Kewaunee, Oshkosh, Cudahy, Fond du Lac, it didn't matter; we grew up feeling special.

We grew up with photos of the Packers. Yes, we watched the games on TV and (if we were lucky) got to an intersquad game now and then, but we always had access to the pictures and we studied them—in the newspaper, in Packer yearbooks, in study hall, after school. We didn't think about the photographer then. It was the players we cared about. Just the same, the words were always there, "Photo by Vernon J. Biever." We came to know the name in the unconcerned way we regarded adults. The governor was Warren Knowles, the Packers' trainer Dominic Gentile, this Biever guy fell somewhere in between.

We grew up and moved away, and I moved east and took a job in book publishing. With each year that passed, the Packers became, more and more, just another fond memory of Wisconsin, a recollection like frozen custard and perch fries, fading like a language you don't use any more, so gradual you don't notice you're forgetting. Luck had it, though, that the house I was working for was publishing a book by Jerry Kramer and Dick Schaap. They needed Packer photographs for illustrations. The words came back without trying to remember. "Photo by Vernon J. Biever."

He sent in a large portfolio folder filled with about twenty-five photos. It was a treasury of historical sports photography, but more than that, they were twenty-five memories. Bart Starr squinting into the low winter sun as he generaled a game-winning drive. Jerry Kramer and Fuzzy Thurston, animate rock slabs leading the Packer sweep. Travis Williams midair, Jim Taylor surging, Ray Nitschke bloodied and raging. Willie Wood's swaggering, Boyd Dowler diving, Lombardi prowling the sidelines.

The day was lost. I closed my door and ignored the phone.

The following morning, resuming employment, I looked at them again, but with a professional eye. The images were only more impressive still. Beyond any personal associations to them, there was no denying the quality of the work. When I was a kid I thought the pictures were great because I was a Packers fan. Now, from the presumably impartial distance of years and a bit more informed by schooling and experience, it was perfectly clear that these were incredible photographs. Maybe I was just a photography fan all along.

Our impressions of art work and historical images differ with each set of eyes, but this is what I saw (and see) in Vernon Biever's work:

Of the millions of fractional movements that make up a sequence of motion—whether a broken-field run, a long pass, or a pile-driving tackle—only a precious few suggest the whole, and it is Biever's rare ability to isolate those vital representative moments. At the same time his compositions are graceful, he finds fluidity in his forms, grouped in dramatically sculptural fashion. In this respect, that these are photographs of football players is almost secondary; like any other accomplished visual work, his photography transcends its subject matter. Compare it to Lewis Wickes Hine's *Steamfitter*. Biever also takes advantage of the extreme weather conditions of the late fall/early winter Upper Midwest, exploiting them to heighten the epic qualities implicit in football games. Here look at Arthur Rothstein's *Dust Storm*, Laura Gilpin's *Washington Square*, and Alfred Steiglitz's *The Hand of Man*.

Biever's candid portraiture is also remarkable. Intimate, never intrusive, his images can be compared to those of Edward Curtis, Dorothea Lange and Walker Evans, quietly exposing elements of character. In Vernon Biever's subjects we see athletes less motivated to play football than compelled.

The match of Vernon Biever and the Green Bay Packers represents a rare pairing of artist and subject ideally suited for each other. Biever combines a talent honed by experience with a respect for his subject to not merely chronicle a team, but to fix the images with an aspect of legend. If the Lombardi years first brought him to national prominence, it is a testimony to his abilities that as much of his greatest work depicts players, teams, and games after Lombardi. And now he has a new generation of Green Bay Packer greats, the 1997 Super Bowl champions. Thirty years from now we'll look at Vernon Biever's photos of today's Green Bay Packers and our memories and imaginations will work the same way, bespeaking his unique talent for perfectly distilling teams, seasons, players, and games into a select collection of images.

It is difficult to isolate any one quality of Vernon Biever's photography as the key to his artistic mastery, and maybe that's the explanation. He orchestrates all of the elements into a single accomplishment. It is often said that baseball is a visually poetic sport. If this is so, then football is visually symphonic, an effort by many to act in accord, drawing a harmony of purpose from the constant of chaos. Vernon Biever is among the most masterful visual interpreters of the score.

The Glory of Titletown began ten years ago with my reacquaintance with Vernon Biever. Because of the photo album nature of it, it includes the recollections, reminiscences, opinions, and stories of players, coaches, administrators, a sports columnist, a broadcaster, and a football filmmaker, who have known Vernon Biever and his work. This book is an appreciation, a tribute, and a celebration of the medium and the sport, a photographer and his subjects.

PETER STRUPP
Cambridge, Massachusetts
February 1997

FOREWORD

It would have to be one of the more difficult sports trivia questions.

Name the Pro Football Hall of Famer whose career began in 1941, whose team has won six NFL championships during his career and has included fifteen other Hall of Famers, who has participated in every Super Bowl game, and who is still active today.

You probably won't hear his name on any of the cable sports channels' talk shows, or on any sports radio stations. No matter how many football games you've seen or for how long you've been a football fan, it's still a tough question. Even some current players on his own team might not be able to come up with the answer.

That answer, of course, is Vernon Biever.

Vernon Biever is a professional sports photographer, covering the Green Bay Packers. Actually, it's more accurate to say that Vernon Biever is *the* Green Bay Packers' photographer. He has been since 1941. When Vernon began, Curley Lambeau was the Packers' head coach. Don Hutson, Clarke Hinkle, and Cecil Isbell were playing, and Tony Canadeo was in his rookie season. Whizzer White was playing for the Lions and Sammy Baugh for the Redskins. Sid Luckman was quarterbacking the Bears. Do you recall the blue and gold "throwback" uniforms the Packers wore a couple years ago as a part of the NFL's 75th Anniversary Season? They were replicas of the uniforms the Packers were actually wearing the year Vernon Biever started photographing games.

The 1941 Packers went 10-1 and came within a divisional playoff (the first in NFL history) of another trip to the championship game. Vernon Biever was nineteen years old, and that was the beginning of a career that has spanned the modern history of professional football. He was with the Packers in 1950, when they put on green and gold for the first time, and in 1957 when we first set foot into the new stadium, which would later be renamed Lambeau Field. Vernon covered the arrival of Vince Lombardi in 1959, Paul Hornung's 176 points in 1960, the 1961 championship over the Giants in Green Bay, and the title rematch a year later at Yankee Stadium. Some of the most famous photographs in sports history are Vernon's shots of the 1965 sudden death playoff against the Colts, the championship in the mud over the Browns that followed it, and then the two NFL titles after that, in Dallas in 1966, and again over the Cowboys in Green Bay in 1967, the famous "ice bowl" game. Of course, there were the first two Super Bowl games as well.

It doesn't end there. There were exciting playoff seasons in 1972 and 1982 and the record-setting season of come-from-behind wins and one-point victories in 1989. Now with this Super Bowl XXXI champion Packer team—his most famous subjects in thirty years—it's almost like it's all just beginning for Vernon. Where he was once photographing Lombardi and numerous future Hall of Famers, Vernon's now covering Mike Holmgren, Reggie White, Brett Favre, and several other very talented performers. These current

Packers took the team back to the Super Bowl, and Vernon was there with them. He's been there all along. Vernon is one of only a handful of photographers to have covered all thirty-one Super Bowl games.

Television is largely credited with the popularization of professional football in the 1950s and 1960s and with its growth into the giant sports and entertainment role it now plays in our society. I think photography, though, also deserves some of the credit. Long before the first televised football game, photography was reporting and recording the game in a very special way for football fans. When we think of Red Grange or Bronko Nagurski or Ernie Nevers, we think of them in photographs from that early era. Photography was the only visual medium of football then, but the fact is that even throughout the rest of the game's history, when we recall players, teams, and games, what we're often remembering are photographs of them. That process continues today with every morning's sports section.

Football teams and football players throughout the history of the NFL have entrusted their images to the photographers who cover the sport. That trust demands a keen knowledge of the game and a deep respect for it, high standards of professionalism and disciplined dedication to the craft. I'm glad to have played for the team that had Vernon Biever as photographer, because he possessed all of these traits and, even more, a lasting level of excellence in his artistry.

If you're still wondering about the Hall of Fame part of the sports trivia question, perhaps I should explain. Vernon is a Pro Football Hall of Fame photographer of the year. His work hangs in the Hall, permanently honored by the sport whose growth he has contributed to over a career of fifty years and counting.

On a personal note, Vernon Biever is one of our family's favorite people. Developing a friendship with him during my years in Green Bay was a huge bonus I will always treasure. He was, and remains, a truly special gentleman. Far more important than his photographic accomplishments are his inner strengths and characteristics. Vernon is the consummate professional. Words such as committed, proud, talented, classy, courteous, and full of integrity and humility only begin to describe this exceptional photographer.

I'm sure you'll enjoy this collection of Vernon Biever's work for many years to come.

BART STARR

The Glory of
TITLETOWN

Vernon Biever. Green Bay, 1957.

Vernon's the greatest. Really is. He's captured the whole deal, I think.

MAX MCGEE

Vernon has taken all these pictures of all these guys in their glory and their humility and their humanity. He caught Lombardi waving a finger or Starr staring down a lineman. He's been there. Yet Vernon has led a normal life. He's been a father and a husband and has run businesses all along. He wasn't a drugstore cowboy running around the world. On a Sunday night he would be going home and on Monday morning opening up the store. He's a pretty normal guy.

GEORGE VECSEY
The New York Times

Vernon was great at it, and he's still going. I see him out around the sidelines, and a lot of times I think, Vernon, now don't get run over and hurt yourself.

MAX MCGEE

That man is a pro, that guy. Vernon knows what he is doing. I remember him on the sidelines, three or four cameras around his neck, hanging in there with plays coming toward him, shooting. But he never got hit, which is more than I can say for Dan Devine. You get your butt out of the way, that's what you do. You got six, seven hundred pounds coming at you, two or three bodies running, you can't stop that. They'll roll you up like a blanket. I can't remember Vernon ever getting caught like that, though. Too quick on his feet. Too wily.

JOHN BROCKINGTON

Hey, taking photos is a very physical act.

GEORGE VECSEY
The New York Times

Don Hutson. Green Bay, 1941.

Don Hutson was a man apart. He was way beyond. In 1942 he catches seventy-four balls, the second guy in the league has twenty-seven. That gives you some idea how good he was. He had everything, size, speed. He was about 6'1", 170 pounds, he'd be a decent sized receiver today. Ran a 9.5 one-hundred. Had big hands, had a great leaping ability, and he was smart. He invented pass patterns. He was remarkable. He played 117 games and scored 105 touchdowns, that's phenomenal. And playing both ways.

He started out also playing defensive end his first four years. Then they drafted a guy named Larry Craig from South Carolina in 1939, and he became what they called "Hutson's Muscle." He went to left end on defense, and Hutson dropped back into the secondary, and Craig played blocking back in the Notre Dame Box on offense. Hutson was a fine defensive back. In fact, I think he only played defensive back from 1939 to 1945, and when he retired from professional football he was number two in the history of the NFL with thirty-nine interceptions. On the defensive side of the ball. Just think of it.

Talk about a guy who dominated the game, he was really something. He also kicked short-range and medium field goals and extra points. I believe that he was the greatest player to have played the game.

LEE REMMEL
Green Bay Packers Executive Director of Public Relations

The Packers back then weren't known as a ground team. The Packers were primarily a great passing team with Hutson and Carl Mulleneaux and other people there. I think they threw the ball more than most of them. Herber was just before my day, but he and Isbell were both great passers. I used to throw it a little bit, but they were the real good passers. I threw single wing in 1943 and '44, but most of the passing was done by Herber, before me, and Cecil when I was there. I played with Don in '41, '42, '43, and, well, coming home in '44 for those furlough games.

TONY CANADEO

Don Hutson is a little bigger than most anybody. There's Don Hutson, and then there's everybody else. I don't care how many of us there are, and I didn't catch as many balls as he did as a Packer, but two or three other guys did, but that doesn't make any difference. There's still Don Hutson and everybody else. And everybody else includes Sterling Sharpe, James Lofton, myself, and everybody. I've seen some film of Hutson, and there wasn't anything wrong with Don Hutson that would have eliminated him from today's picture as a player. First of all, he was a bigger guy than most people would really realize coming out of those years. He was well over six feet, and a pretty lanky guy, and he could run like the wind. He wouldn't have to apologize to anyone for his speed and quickness.

BOYD DOWLER

Ted Fritsch. Green Bay, 1942.

In 1941 I went up to St. Norbert College in DePere, near Green Bay. Before going, I stopped in at the *Milwaukee Sentinel* to talk to the sports editor, Stoney McGlynn. The way they had been getting pictures of Packer games was by sending a staff photographer up to Green Bay and back by car. They would miss the first deadlines.

I said, "You know I'll be in that area and I can take pictures," —out of my high school camera club, you know— "so why send a photographer up there? Save some money. And time. I'll put the film on the train after the game, the Northwestern, and I'll call you and tell you who's got the film, what conductor and what car, and you pick it up."

He said, "There's a game next Sunday, the Packers are playing the Bears. Do what you can do."

After I sent the film in, that first night I couldn't sleep. What did I get? First thing in the morning, I rushed down to the local drug store and picked up a *Sentinel*, and they had a pretty good spread of pictures. They ran maybe three.

So I continued. When they played in Milwaukee, I wouldn't take them. I'd listen to the game on the radio. There wasn't any television in those years. And of course, away games I didn't take either. After about two years, I went in the service. I was an army photographer over in Germany and France with the 100th Infantry Division.

When I came back, the *Sentinel*, the *Journal*, the AP, and UPI all had gotten together, and now they chartered a plane up to Green Bay on game days. I was out of business. I went to the Packers and spoke with the team's PR guy then, Jug Earpe, who had been a player, and said, "How about doing this work for you? You want a record of your games; give me a field pass and I'll give you some pictures."

Teams didn't have photographers at that time. I think I was the first one. That's how the whole thing started.

VERNON BIEVER

Ted Fritsch was home grown. From Sparta, Wisconsin, if I remember correctly. He went to what was then called Central State Teacher's College, now UW Stevens Point. He was a very talented athlete, you know. He played major league basketball, in the National Basketball League, as a guard with the Oshkosh All-Stars, of Oshkosh, Wisconsin. He played for them, and he played triple-A baseball with the Toledo Mudhens. And I think he might have played on the Pacific Coast League. And of course he was an all-league fullback with the Packers. Led the league in scoring in 1946. The team had 148 points that season; he had 100 of them. Not bad. He was big strong guy, but he was a bane of Curley Lambeau's existence because he was always overweight. Curley was always penalizing him for being overweight. He was a big, happy-go-lucky guy. Didn't have a mean bone in his body.

LEE REMMEL
Green Bay Packers Executive Director of Public Relations

Ted was a great football player. He was a comical guy too, kept us all loose. But he was a good football player.

TONY CANADEO

I didn't play in the 1944 championship game at the Polo Grounds because I was already back in England. See, I came home on furlough when my first son was born in '44. I played three games with the Packers because we told the army that my wife had a relapse. I ended up playing three ballgames with 'em. That was in October, I believe. I played against the Cleveland Rams and the Detroit Lions in Detroit, and I played at Wrigley Field against the Chicago Bears. And I took the train back to El Paso, Texas, and shipped back from there.

TONY CANADEO

I came from Notre Dame, with Knute Rockne and the great tradition that was there too, so I bought right into the pride of the Packers. To me it wasn't like playing pro football, it wasn't a business. It was more of an extension of Notre Dame, playing in a small town atmosphere, and I loved it. It was a lot to live up to. It was a trying time, but it was an exciting time too. And it stretches you; you grow.

MIKE McCOY

We played an intersquad game on Thanksgiving in 1949. Those were lean money years. They raised a little dough that day to pay salaries for the rest of the year. It was the only intersquad game, I think, that no one hit the ground.

TONY CANADEO

Tony Canadeo. Green Bay, 1949.

Larry Coutre. Green Bay, 1950.

To me, that was always my Super Bowl, playing the Bears. The players disliked each other, being just down the road, it's just one of the all-time great rivalries in sports. I mean, players truly, truly disliked each other. Outside of the game, you might do business with each other, you might be friends, you might get Christmas cards, but come the Sunday of the Packers and Bears, there's animosity. I mean, I like Mark Bortz and Jay Hilgenberg and Tom Thayer, I played against them for nine years. Eighteen games against those guys. We shake hands, we're buddy-buddies and all that, but when we line up to play, look out because somebody's going to get the tar knocked out of them. And we'll laugh after we do it. We laugh at each other, but when the ball's snapped, look out. There were some great, great individual battles in there. The games were fun. Some of my fondest memories come from the Bears games.

Brian Noble

The rivalries aren't just the fans'. They exist, especially against the Bears. There's so much tradition in that game. The fans will never let the rivalry die in that game. When we're at a grocery store somebody might come up and say, "Y'all do anything, just make sure you beat the Bears again." The players, we get into that.

Edgar Bennett

Everybody had to play well because the Bears were going to take your head off. It was just a physical game. And the best team didn't necessarily have to win, you know, in that series. You understand what I'm saying.

Willie Wood

Billy Grimes. Green Bay, 1951.

I remember one time we went and practiced over there at the old stadium. I was pleased that I didn't have to play there. It was like going back to high school, which is what it was.

WILLIE WOOD

In Vernon Biever's working career, the Green Bay Packers became and have remained a viable team in professional football. And Vernon, a modest guy, not a pretentious person, became an important part of that team, and he's remained that.

You really could make a case that in his lifetime he's an embodiment of the survival, then growing sophistication, and ultimately the worldliness of the Packers. Vernon started out as a college kid who talked his way in. They were then playing in a pretty rudimentary league, and in his lifetime he wound up jetting to Super Bowls.

GEORGE VECSEY
The New York Times

For the history of the team, for the way that the community and the team are associated, if you want to talk about America's team, you need look no further than the Green Bay Packers.

JERRY KRAMER

Fred Cone. Milwaukee, 1952.

There were maybe four or five photographers covering games then. We wanted more on the sidelines with us to kneel alongside and cut the wind a little. With our old cameras, 4x5 Speed Graphics, we couldn't take very many pictures of the game. We had to prefocus a certain spot on the field and hope for the action to come there. We had to wait. So you might take six or eight; ten would be an exception. By the nature of that equipment, a kind of discipline was forced on us. It was good training in learning how to anticipate action. You could practice your knowledge of football. You learned to be precise. You had to learn to really wait until you thought it was the exact time to snap the shutter.

VERNON BIEVER

I sort of felt Green Bay was the right place for me. Of course, I didn't know where Green Bay was. I knew it was in Wisconsin, but, you know, I had never been to Wisconsin. I got a little concerned when we couldn't fly directly into Green Bay. We flew into Chicago and caught that North Central, you know, which was one of those little prop jobs, and I got a little concerned. I said, "Where in the heck am I?" We got to Green Bay, and at that time the airport looked like one of those little substations someplace, you know, a little metal building for an airport. Coming out of L.A. or D.C., well, it was sort of a culture shock, I guess you might say, for me. But at the time it really didn't matter that much. My purpose of coming there was to make the team, and that was what I was focusing in on, and anything else that happened around me, you understand, was just coincidental.

WILLIE WOOD

Floyd "Breezy" Reid. Green Bay, 1953.

We played the 49ers for the very first time in 1950, Gene Ronzani's first year as head coach of the Packers. We played over in old City Stadium on the East Side. I can still see Paul Christman hit Breezy Reid down the south sideline for a touchdown in the last minute of play, and the Packers won the game, 25-21.

LEE REMMEL
Green Bay Packers Executive Director of Public Relations

Breezy was a very good back, you know, he just played on a lousy ball club. He had very good quickness. And all those older guys, they were pretty tough. The guys I played with in '54 and '55 were the old group—the changeover. It was right in that transitional period, where the old guys chewed tobacco and would spit on your hands and peed on you in the showers. But that's the kind of guys they were, just hell raisers, you know, and didn't make much money. Just tickled to death to be there. And that's the kind of guy Breezy was. Tough as nails, but just had a good time.

GARY KNAFELC

If you're going to be there and want to do a good job, then you'd just as soon really be a hard ass about it. That was my attitude playing. You're going to suffer and hurt, but you'd just as soon try and knock somebody else out as them knocking you out. So it was dog eat dog.

JIM TAYLOR

Billy Howton. Green Bay, 1954.

My last year was Bill Howton's rookie year. Bill Howton was a great pass receiver, a great receiver. Especially as Tobin Rote developed into a great quarterback.

TONY CANADEO

Bill Howton was my roommate and undoubtedly the best ballplayer we had, a great receiver. And he was, more or less, the self-proclaimed leader of our team. He called me one day just after Lombardi arrived and said, "Could you meet me at the airport? I'm flying in to see Vince."

This was the day after I saw him, and I said, "Well, first of all, I sure wouldn't call him Vince. And secondly, I'd be very cautious . . ."

"Oh, no, no, no, there's not a problem. He wants to see me, and I just want to get there and set him straight as to what we have to do to be a winner."

I said, "I would suggest you just go in there and listen."

He said, "Oh, no, no problem. Pick me up, take me over there. Vince and I are going to have lunch, and I'll stick around for a while, and then maybe you and I can have dinner."

I said that would be fine. I picked him up, took him down, that was on Washington Street, dropped him off. He went inside. My wife had asked me to go over to Prange's to pick up something, and I couldn't have been gone maybe fifteen or twenty minutes, but by the time I got home my wife said that Bill Howton had called and wanted me to come down and pick him up, that he has to go back to Dallas right away. I couldn't figure out what it was, so I drove down.

He was standing outside waiting for me.

I said, "What happened to your lunch?"

"Well, never mind, something came up, and I have to go back to Dallas right away."

He was very quiet. Didn't say a word. I took him back to the airport and he flew out. Next day I read in the paper that he had been traded to Cleveland.

I never found out what he said or what happened, and he never told me. He probably went in and said Vince-this and Vince-that and, bingo, he was gone.

Billy was probably one of the best pass receivers to ever play the game. He still holds a league record. And he was the first guy that Lombardi cut. He was making a statement. No one ever disagreed with him. All of us knew then, if he's getting rid of our best player, boy, this guy is serious. All of us knew exactly where we stood. That's the kind of guy he was.

GARY KNAFELC

Gary Knafelc. Green Bay, 1955.

That game was against Detroit in the old City Stadium, East High School. I don't care what football players say, they love to have people talking to them. They say they don't like it; I loved it. I still love it. If these guys say they don't, they're lying, it's a bunch of baloney.

GARY KNAFELC

I just couldn't turn a kid down. I couldn't. There were times when we had two-a-days. After the first practice, the kids would all be out there with their little helmets and pieces of paper, and they're looking at you like you're something really special, and they want autographs. And it was very hard for me to sign a few and say I've got to go. It just broke my heart, because, you know, I had to go, I had to catch a bus. So what I started doing was, I said, "Tell you what, everybody just line up on my right, nice orderly fashion," and I'd sign all the autographs. Sometimes there would be so many kids there that all the other players would have gone back to the locker room, showered, got dressed, got on the bus to go back to DePere, I was still on the field signing. They'd say, "See you later, Brock! See you later!"

But I just couldn't turn them down, because you don't know where they're going to be the next day. Their families might have just come through for a minute, watched the Packer practice, then they had to go someplace else. And I also knew, what the heck, it isn't going to be like this for the rest of my life. One of these days, hey, they won't want my autograph. I just didn't like turning down kids.

I guess everybody has a different spin on being a pro, you know. Some say, "I don't owe anybody anything," and I guess they don't. But they do. Especially with little kids. It's part of the territory that you assume when you become a pro. Those kids come out there, and to them, you are it. I mean, it's like looking at Mickey Mouse to them, except that Mickey Mouse can't hold a candle to a Packer in Green Bay.

JOHN BROCKINGTON

Tobin Rote. Green Bay, 1950.

They shouldn't forget that this league was built in the 1950s and '60s, a lot of it. You tried to help build the game, and you did. Our Packer team did. You tried to help make a great league and make football great, and you paid some dues being a part of it.

JIM TAYLOR

Tobin Rote would play today. Tobin would have been a great star in today's football. Probably the toughest quarterback I've ever seen. He could throw the ball, he could run, had the meanest attitude you've ever seen, was a great competitor. He firmly believed, and he had to at that time probably, that if the team wouldn't win the game he'd do it all by myself. And he could do it. He was a fantastic quarterback. Very similar to Favre. I've saw Tobin come back to the huddle where he couldn't even see. We played several games where he had a broken nose, and he kept right on. We didn't have face masks, you know, just that one little bar.

GARY KNAFELC

Tobin Rote was very tough. I remember one time he had his nose broken against the Bears, and he came right back in on the next play. He just went out for one play and was back in. He was one of the toughest football players God ever made. And a fine football player. He was a big guy, 6'3", 220. He could throw the ball, and he was a fine runner. He was our leading rusher for three years.

LEE REMMEL
Green Bay Packers Executive Director of Public Relations

I think if you forget where you came from, you forget what you are supposed to be all about. I think the league has lost some of that. Some of these guys don't realize where the league came from, and the blood and guts that went into building it.

SEAN JONES

Al Carmichael, Forrest Gregg. Milwaukee, 1956.

The Lombardi Era made for the Packer team a place in football history that will never be forgotten.

FUZZY THURSTON

You don't want to deal with the Packer legacy, but you have to deal with it. And the only way you're going to get it out of your mind is to win a Super Bowl.

ROBERT BROOKS

People never forget about the old years. The stamp of those glory years is firmly in place.

BRIAN NOBLE

You see, I'm still coming from the old school. You watch these runners and these punt returners today. They always head for the sidelines, and the first time somebody comes, they step out of bounds. You never heard of that in my day. You cut back on the field, and the extra four yards you get there might put you over the goal line. So there's a different mentality. Now they make a lot of money. To us, we were bodies, and you threw your body on the line. You know, to play the game well I think you have to play that way. So I'm not much for the way they pass rules to save quarterbacks and all that stuff. I say let 'em play. What the hell.

MAX MCGEE

Football's still four downs and ten yards. That doesn't change. What has changed are the rules. Offensive linemen don't have to keep their hands in around their chest to block, so they block more like Sumo wrestlers; push-shove is their game. The guys are a lot bigger, a lot heavier, a mass-weight that's difficult to move. It used to be fitness.

DONNY ANDERSON

Gary Knafelc, Dave Hanner. Green Bay, 1961.

It's amazing, but that picture's been all over. One time a Dallas paper had a survey for the best football picture of the year of an individual, and everybody had all sorts of these pictures, but there it was. They had it there.

That photographer always had different innovations and he was the only one who did anything different. If you look at those old bubble gum cards, you just stood there flat-footed and held the ball out, and they took a picture of you, and you looked like you were just some kind of a clone. It was ugly. But he came along and did all these different things. He asked me to dive like that, and I said sure. He threw the ball, and I dived.

GARY KNAFELC

I watched the video of that Tampa Bay game the other day. My picture was on the ticket for that game. We had almost 500 yards total offense. I think they had fifty-six yards. It came on the screen that over two feet of snow had fallen and that only 19,000 people showed up for that game. I keep telling my wife that there are 30,000 tickets out there somewhere with my picture on it, all those people who stayed home.

MARK MURPHY

Most present day football cards are action photos, or if they take a shot of you it's on the sidelines without your helmet on. I posed for a couple cards, but nothing like the swinging through the air they did then. Nowadays, I don't know how many athletes would do that.

The thing that bothers me today is that back when those old football card photos were done, they were collectibles not because of their dollar value but because kids just liked to say they had one of those cards. Now it's gotten to the point that there's such a large value placed on those things that it's really spoiled for the kid that just wants to have a Reggie White autographed football card or a Brett Favre autographed football. It's upsetting to the extent that the days of Reggie and Brett walking to camp are over, because you have people paying young kids to run up there and get their autograph and they pay the kids five, ten bucks, then turn around and sell the thing for sixty, seventy dollars. It's ruined something very memorable for a kid.

BRIAN NOBLE

We usually kind of liked picture day because it was toward the end of two-a-days and it took one half of a day. So we did these pre-posed pictures to make them look like action shots, and missed a practice by doing so. It was a fun deal.

DONNY ANDERSON

Vince Lombardi. Green Bay, 1961.

He came in and just set down, set the rules down and said well this is the way it's going to be, and we're going to be early for meetings and we're going to be punctual. He was like a drill sergeant. You just knew there wasn't any double or triple standards, just one set of rules and everybody went by them. No favorites and there's no partiality, which was good, it's what I like. Nothing wishy-washy, all business. I got on very well with him. You admired him and respected him. He didn't talk out of both sides of his mouth, give you any song and dance.

JIM TAYLOR

I first met Lombardi when came into town, one night at the hockey arena. They were watching a hockey game. He had just first come into town that night. He asked to see me tomorrow morning, he said, at nine o'clock. I said okay. I went down to see him.

I always liked to tell stories and jokes, and I thought I was kind of clever, so when he said, "How much do you weigh?" I lied and said 225.

He said, "Well, then you're going to be my tight end next year."

I looked at him, and I kind of laughed, and I said, "Coach, I haven't hit anybody in five years."

He said, "Then where would you like to be traded?"

I said, "You just found yourself a hell of a tight end."

He scared the hell out of me. From then on I knew I couldn't mess with him at all. I was physically afraid of the man. Scared me to death.

GARY KNAFELC

The coach-player relationship hasn't really changed over the years. There are the obvious things. The guys are making a lot more money now. And since I've been coaching, certainly since I was a player, you have to explain to a player why you're doing something more often. Thirty years ago, the coach-player relationship was one where the coach would say, "I want you to run around the building fourteen times," and you just did it. You just got up and did it. Now, if you wanted them to do that you'd better have pretty good reasons why. And then they'd do it, but you've got to be able to explain why. The actual coach-and-player relationship, however, I'm sure is similar, very similar.

MIKE HOLMGREN

At the time I didn't know anything about the Lombardi tirades, for lack of a better word. He was dressed up I guess when we first met, so his personality fit the outfit. When we got to camp and he started talking his talk, the first time he addressed the whole team, he was kind of telling you what he expected of his men. That was fine. I was used to that, all the coaches said that. What I didn't realize was that he also had the ability to give you the tongue lashing, that we grew to love and understand, you might say. It got to a point where it became very frightening, and I would say to myself, "I certainly don't want this guy on my butt." For the longest time, hell, I just kind of stayed away from him.

And I stayed away from everybody. I just went and played football, did my job, and did not try to be one of the boys. A lot of the rookies in camp, they want to be buddy-buddy with the veterans, but the veterans don't have any part of that. The guys who want to be buddy-buddy seem to be the ones that they always finger out to play these dirty tricks on. So I just kind of stayed away from everybody.

WILLIE WOOD

From playing with the Packers I still have my watch fifteen minutes fast. If a meeting was at 3:00, everybody was there at 2:45. That was Lombardi Time, and I'm still on Lombardi Time. Playing with those guys at a young age like I was, it really gave me a great foundation to my life. Being a part of the Green Bay Packer organization developed my life. Having a leader like Lombardi and having all the leaders on the team. I mean, we didn't have stars, we had leaders. And being a Green Bay Packer, you knew that everybody was chomping at the bit, "When is it my turn to make the big play?" We need people who stand up and want to be counted. We don't need those people who stay in the background. You need people like that who want to do it, and we had it.

MARV FLEMING

I came to Green Bay after a season with the Colts, and before 1959 there were a lot of differences. Baltimore was number one, the world champions, and Green Bay was in last place. The Colts had All-Pros with Unitas, Moore, Ameche, Berry, Marchetti, Donovan, etc. The Packers had none. Both the Colts and Packers had great coaches, with Lombardi becoming the best of all time. Lombardi put that team into high gear and produced five world championships and twelve members of the Pro Football Hall of Fame: himself, Adderley, Davis, Gregg, Hornung, Jordan, Nitschke, Ringo, Starr, Taylor, Tunnell, and Wood. The Colts were great, the Packers the greatest.

FUZZY THURSTON

I look at Lombardi and all the great players he coached and what successful people they are outside of football. Every interview I ever heard from those guys, they'll always tell you they think about Vince Lombardi every day. What kind of person gets in your head that way? That's what I think of when I think of Lombardi. What kind of man drove people to succeed beyond what people expected them to do?

SEAN JONES

Vince Lombardi, Jim Weatherwax, Lee Roy Caffey,
Dave Robinson, Paul Hornung Max McGee, Boyd Dowler,
Bart Starr, Bob Skoronski, Forrest Gregg. Dallas, 1967.

Vince Lombardi. Milwaukee, 1967.

Vince had that ability to sit you down and let you know the importance your being ready to play for a particular ball game.

About the time of that first intersquad game I kind of wrenched my knee, and it was swollen. Vince walked up to me and said, "If you expect to play football for the Green Bay Packers, you'll be ready to play next week."

And I said, "Well, yes sir," you know.

My knee at that time was about as big as my head. So I had the trainer spend a lot of time to try and get the swelling out. And it worked; it fell in place. But the knees are full of arthritis now.

WILLIE WOOD

I remember when Zeke Bratkowski came from the Rams to the Packers. We were having practice and we were running pass patterns, and he'd take the snap and run back really quick and throw the ball. And, like, nobody was ready. The receivers just got off the line and were going to make their move, and the ball was in the air already, you know. This happened one time, two times, and after the third time Lombardi says, "Wait, stop, stop."

He says, "Zeke, take your time, you're not with the Rams anymore. You've got lots . . . of . . . time."

MARV FLEMING

It was a tough camp, a hard camp. Being one of the lighter offensive linemen, I always kind of had it in the back of my head that some of these big guys were going to drop long before I do. You're sitting over there and you're looking at big Ron Kostelnick who's tipping the scales at about 285 trying to do these up-downs, and you're at 235 and you're popping up pretty good, and you think, if he's going to kill me, they'd better get the ambulance ready for a lot of other people first.

But rather than the up-downs and the pure hell of training camp, the more impressive thing about Lombardi was his ability to speak, his ability to arouse people, or to inform people. What I remember most was the initial session and several evening sessions with Coach Lombardi when he was talking about the Green Bay Packers and their tradition and what an honor it was to play for this team that had been one of the founders of the National Football League. He really had an ability to talk, to be an orator.

KEN BOWMAN

I'm just glad I played when I played. I'm glad I had an opportunity to be with Coach Lombardi and be a part of that Packer team.

JIM TAYLOR

Vince Lombardi, Bart Starr. Green Bay, 1966.

I know that Lombardi respected Bart Starr a great deal. You know in that Ice Bowl game, he called the time out and went over to talk to Coach Lombardi, and he said to him that he was thinking about running a quarterback sneak. And Lombardi told Bart, "It's cold out here. Just get the damn thing in the end zone and let's get out of here." He trusted him to that extent.

KEN BOWMAN

Lombardi saw in Vernon someone that he respected, and knew that he was a professional, and gave him access to his team. You knew right away with Vernon that there was a certain class and integrity to everything that he did.

STEVE SABOL
NFL Films

The history of the Packers and Vernon's career go hand in hand. He understands their position in the sports world and his growth has been right along with theirs. He was there when the high moments came along with Coach Lombardi. And I think that being a good photographer is understanding the person you're shooting as well. Any of us who were around Coach Lombardi realized that it was good to get him at the right moment if you were going to interview him or take his picture or shoot anything along the sidelines. Vernon knew it all along.

JIM IRWIN
WTMJ Radio

While an insider, Vernon also embodied the community, but that isn't to say he was your average fan. Vernon knew the players and coaches. I can still hear him talking about Lombardi and Starr. But he wasn't an insider in the sense that he would identify with them. To Vernon the team is bigger than the individuals. His real identification was with the team, with the Green Bay Packers as a cultural presence in the state and a team that he loved beyond his work, loved the fact of them. I wouldn't call Vernon a fan as much as I would just say that he's a Wisconsinite, a citizen of the state, and the Packers are part of that identity. In that regard, Vernon's a sort of personification of the state's relationship with that team.

GEORGE VECSEY
The New York Times

Vince Lombardi. Green Bay, 1967.

As far as building the image of the Green Bay Packers goes, Vernon's certainly been up to the task. You think of the great images in the history of football photography, the blood trickling down Y.A. Tittle's head, Ameche with that huge hole opening before him, and Vernon's shots of the steam of the breath of the Cowboys and Packers, these things contributed to forming the image of the game. Vernon's probably had as much to do—more to do with—well, can you name a single print journalist who has had more impact on knowing the Green Bay Packers?

GEORGE VECSEY
The New York Times

Lombardi's words to the press in his office after the Ice Bowl were, "It took all of our poise, all of our experience to win the game."

LEE REMMEL
Green Bay Packers Executive Director of Public Relations

The thing I remember after that game was Ray Nitshcke's toes were gray. Mine had some frostbite right on the tips. I was sitting there with my toes in an ice bucket, because that's how they treated frostbite, but I looked over at him and his damn toes, they were gray all the way back to the fat part of his foot, and I thought this guy might be in the market to lose any couple of toes here. But Ray had a tower fall on him, for cripes sake, and that didn't stop him.

KEN BOWMAN

We never really had to play in ice or snow, only in the playoff games. You know everybody always remembers Green Bay as the ice house and all that, and the game against Dallas, but you know if you played in Chicago in January it would be just as bad. The only reason that they don't bitch about Chicago and Minnesota and all the rest of the teams at that time is that they weren't in the playoffs, see.

PAUL HORNUNG

Vince Lombardi, Jerry Kramer. Miami, 1968.

There was something said like on Wednesday or Thursday during the week. The middle of the week Coach Lombardi said something like, "This might be our last game together." Didn't say anything more. Just said that and went on. I know it caused us to look at each other and look around a little bit. So it planted the possibility. And he didn't elaborate, didn't discuss it any more, and that was all that I had heard. That's the only thing that I knew. But I think it opened up our minds to the possibility.

I don't know if Lombardi's deal with Washington was already in motion at that point. I've pondered that question a time or two and I wouldn't be surprised, let me put it that way. It would be an intelligent thing to do, and Coach Lombardi was certainly intelligent. There wasn't much opportunity in Green Bay, wasn't much that he could ever have a piece of. The security of the family, the hard facts of life are and were that he could get a piece of the team if he went to Washington. Now, had it been in place for a while? I wouldn't have been surprised at all.

JERRY KRAMER

I don't think we knew at all that it would be Vince's last game. I don't know if he had announced that. Anyway, I don't really recall, but I don't remember it as playing "let's get the last one for Vince." I knew it was going to be the last one for me.

We may have had a feeling. It think Vince was aware that the boys were getting old. Time to look for something else. You know, Vince, who I loved and had a great relationship with, I think egowise he might have thought that that was a good time to step out, you know. Three in a row, three NFLs, nobody'd ever won ever. He obviously deserved to have some ownership somewhere, and I think that is why he made the move.

MAX McGEE

It was his due to be carried off the field by his players. It would have been certainly just as appropriate if Bart and Forrest, or Bart and Jimmy, or Bart and Paul, or any of his players had done it. It was just that Forrest and I were standing there, and I said, "Let's give him a ride."

JERRY KRAMER

Vince Lombardi. Green Bay, 1965.

Lombardi changed our whole lives. Everybody up there, we were headed for oblivion.

The Packers my first two years, I think we won four games or something, something ridiculous. So it wasn't the spot to be until he arrived.

PAUL HORNUNG

I wasn't one of his whipping boys, which was good. I think I learned very quickly that you do things his way, and you do them right, which was his way. Mentally, more than anything else. You know, everybody makes physical mistakes, but the things he wouldn't stand for were mental errors. Errors of omission or just doing something totally wrong, he couldn't handle that. I was pretty disciplined mentally, and I'd been raised to steer clear of those things anyway, so I didn't have a whole lot of problem. I kind of thrived on it really.

BOYD DOWLER

I've often been asked to compare Lombardi and Paul Brown. The organizations were similar for how both cities loved their team. Paul Brown was already a legend in Cleveland. He had been successful in the old AAFC, and he came in the NFL and had success that continued there for a number of years.

Paul Brown was, by anyone's evaluation, a coach ahead of his time. Much of the organization, much of the system, much of playing the game more scientifically, all of these things find their way back to Cleveland and an association with Paul Brown.

Coach Lombardi admitted to me on several occasions that there were several things that he actually adopted from Paul Brown. One was the timing of the practice, moving us in such a way where you didn't stay out there forever. You got just a ton done, and it was through a timing element. You didn't have much down time. I would say that over the years we probably practiced less than most teams. But when we were out there, we had very few down moments.

When I came to the Packers, Lombardi had spent '59 there, and they had made a significant turn for the better, compared to what had been there for the decade or more before then. The Browns were already operating from a standpoint of achieved success. But surely, at the end of the Lombardi Era, I was looking back and saying, boy, this guy is everything you'd ever want and need in a coach. Whether you were player, fan, or anyone who had the game at heart.

WILLIE DAVIS

My rookie year, 1959, was a good time to arrive, a good time to be born. I had always played for coaches that were demanding, even in high school. And my dad had been a coach, so I was not as stranger to discipline, and I was not a stranger to coaches that were perfectionist-type people and that sort of thing. There was a little bit of personality adjustment when you come in, Vince being such a strong personality, and, you know, you kind of had to get used to that voice and his, well, let's say he was direct. You had to kind of get used to that or it could shake you up a little bit.

BOYD DOWLER

Paul Hornung. Green Bay, 1957.

When I met Hornung I went to training camp in Winston-Salem, North Carolina, or whichever state it's in. That's when I got out of the service. I had missed two years in the service, and it took me a year to get my timing back after I returned, so I really missed some prime years.

I immediately went to Winston-Salem, and I ran over and I said, "Where's the poker game?"

They said, "It's over in that room."

And I go in there, and there's Hawg Hanner, Bill Forester, and Hornung. Now, normally we didn't let rookies in, but Hornung was already in there. So I'm back in my familiar spot, and that's where we decided, hell, we'd probably make pretty good roommates. Plus he had all the money. Not only was he the bonus plum, but he was winning all the money in the poker game.

MAX McGEE

It was a great little stadium, and Green Bay was glad to have it. I remember Vice President Nixon came up and dedicated the stadium. We all met him. He was on the practice field. I had been at a couple of dinners at the Washington Touchdown Club. We said hello standing out on the field.

PAUL HORNUNG

I caught the last touchdown in the old stadium and the first touchdown in the new stadium in 1959. Dedication Day. We played the Bears, and Babe Parilli scrambled and threw the touchdown pass to me in the end zone that won the game with about a minute and a half to go. Vice President Nixon was there for the dedication, and James Arness, you know, the big cowboy star, and Miss America, Marilyn Van der Burr.

Now Marilyn Van der Burr was from Colorado and had gone to the University of Colorado; in fact, when I was in school I used to date her. So I'm telling everybody, you know, my gal is coming and I'll introduce you and all that kind of stuff. Al Carmichael was on our ball club, from USC, and Al was the kind of guy that no matter what you did, he could better it, see. I don't care what it was. If you broke a hip, he was playing with a fractured back. If you had a fractured back, he had a broken neck. It was that kind of stuff. So I'm telling Al that I'll introduce him to Miss America.

And he said, "Well, Dick and I are very close friends."

I said, "Dick who?"

"Dick Nixon."

And I go, "Oh, c'mon Al, geez."

So now, you've got to picture this. The game is over. Gary Knafelc caught the touchdown pass against the Bears, of all people, to win the game. Al Carmichael and I are in the showers together. We're some of the last few because they had been interviewing us and all that stuff, and we hear this noise and we hear that Richard Nixon is coming into the locker room. Naturally he wants to see me, you know, because I caught the winning touchdown. Nixon sticks his head in the shower. Carmichael is standing beside to me.

Nixon says, "Hey Al! Al! C'mon out here!"

It just killed me.

GARY KNAFELC

Paul Hornung. Green Bay, 1961.

I've always had a tremendous amount of admiration and respect for Vernon Biever and his work. He was never just taking shots, he was making pictures. And that's why, to me, he's the standard-bearer of professional football photography.

Vernon and NFL Films grew as artists during the time of Lombardi's Packers, probably the most romantic team of legend in the history of football. I think they're at the point where they might have surpassed Knute Rockne's Notre Dame teams and the Four Horsemen. And Vernon preserved the images of Lombardi and the Packers better than any other photographer. He captured that team. If Vince Lombardi was the patron saint of professional football, Vernon Biever is the Michaelangelo.

He's influenced work that we have done. I can remember going to our cameramen and showing those shots that he got on the bench and saying, "Now, why can't we get a shot like this. Why aren't we getting shots of Forrest Gregg with his helmet all caked in mud or Paul Hornung with globs or earth stuck in his helmet. Why aren't we getting a shot like this of Lombardi?"

The thing about Vernon is that not only is he a journalist, he's an artist. And he could do both in the same game. You would see shots where he would capture the great plays, the heart of the action, the crisis point. And in that same game he'd have a shot of Lombardi in his rain cap with his lips pursed or a shot of Hornung and Lombardi talking together and you knew just by looking at that picture how Lombardi thought and cared about Hornung. Or a picture of Lombardi yelling at Jerry Kramer, and Lombardi would have those teeth that looked like a mouth full of tombstones. Vernon captured not only the technical brilliance of that team, he also got the emotion.

STEVE SABOL
NFL Films

If you want to really chronicle a game, it requires shots other than just action. You've got to look for that sideline shot that tells the story. You have to look for action as well, you want to be there for the important touchdown, but I also like to watch the sidelines. You have to know your place, but in front of the bench you can do more observant work. The team allows me to do it, and I'm familiar to the players so they are comfortable with my presence.

VERNON BIEVER

Paul Hornung. Milwaukee, 1965.

I always had a pretty good day against the Colts, I don't know why. It just looked like the offense was geared against the Colt defense that way. I didn't play the fourth quarter; they had substituted everybody. We all could have gone another quarter, but we were ahead, easily ahead, so he took everybody out. Lombardi came up to me after that game and he said, "If I knew you were that close to the record I would have left you in." I didn't realize I was close to the record anyway. Forty points was the record.

PAUL HORNUNG

Fuzzy would do whatever he had to do to get the block done, to get the job done. He'd get the guy he was supposed to block. I really admire that kind of tenacity in Fuzzy because he was just a whale of fighter. If you graded the films out and you weren't looking for pretty blocks, you were looking for who got their man, I think Fuzzy probably graded out just as well as Jerry in most of the games.

KEN BOWMAN

Paul Hornung. Green Bay, 1964.

They had a bonus pick then. I knew I was either going to go to the Packers or the Chicago Cardinals, who also had a chance in the bonus pick. The Packers and the Cardinals were the only two teams left. I knew that whoever won the flip, I was going to be their pick because I had been contacted by both teams. I was hoping, honestly, that the Cardinals would win it because with Notre Dame being so close to Chicago, there was already such a fan base there. And as far as marketing purposes were concerned, especially back in those days, going into professsional football in Chicago would have been better. If I had ended up with the Chicago Cardinals, it certainly would have been a different career. It sure wouldn't have been any good for Paul Hornung.

PAUL HORNUNG

Taylor was a good pass receiver, and Hornung was unusual coming out of the backfield. He wasn't speedy, quick and fast, or anything, but boy, he knew where to go and he had good hands and he made plays. He had great instinct for the passing game.

BOYD DOWLER

I couldn't write the script any better for me.

PAUL HORNUNG

Jim Taylor. New York, 1962.

Yankee Stadium in the middle of December, the championship game there, that was the worst game I've ever played in my life.

PAUL HORNUNG

That was probably the most brutal football game that I had ever been in. I know that it was. The weather was terrible, and the field was frozen, and the wind in Yankee Stadium was just terrible. It really was the coldest that I ever played in. The weather affected me more than the Ice Bowl game that was played in Green Bay. We had humiliated the Giants the year before, and they were playing in their own back yard, and they went after it. It was just a real tough game, the way football should be played. Playing it, and watching it now, it was the most physical game that I've ever seen.

RAY NITSCHKE

I had cut my tongue and was kind of bleeding. And I had a elbow that had five or six stitches in it at halftime because it had split open, and they just stitched it up and taped it up. I ended up I think with thirty-one carries, my career high. Under those conditions. I guess it was like twenty, twenty-five below zero the whole ball game. Thirty-one carries that I had, trying to keep it on the ground with the wind and the cold. We didn't have gloves then either. We played with the real elements. It was frigid.

The field was okay probably the first quarter, but then it froze over and it got like glass. I had a lot of times where I was knocked out of bounds because you couldn't cut very well and get up the field. They were roughing me up. They were piling on and stuff. I could take you back and show you if we had the right footage of the out of bounds plays. It would be just like hitting the quarterback when he was throwing the ball, and then they'd rough you up and lay on. They tried to agitate you and all that cheap stuff instead of being a man and hitting you while you're up.

I think I scored the last rushing touchdown in the fourth quarter. It was 9-7, and I'd run a cutback play of some sort, and Sam Huff had overrun it. We had a big opening back to the other side of the field and I cut back, I think it was eight or ten yards, for touchdown. Sam had busted me up pretty good all during the game, and the whole time he'd told me that I stunk. After I was in the end zone with the winning touchdown, I held up the ball and said, "How do I smell from here, Sam?"

JIM TAYLOR

Taylor clearly got the best of that deal, I would think. Taylor was a tough nut. I remember the time Huff kind of hit him out of bounds on that frozen turf, cut his elbow up and all that kind of stuff, and Taylor didn't blink. He was as tough as they came. And still hard as a rock.

MAX McGEE

It had snowed the night before and they had a helicopter come in to stir up all the snow off the seats. The field was pretty snowy, I guess, and covered. Wet, sloppy. Our defense, Nitschke and them, always played tough against Jim Brown. They always rose up to the occasion. It was just a hard fought game that you really enjoyed and really looked forward to, competing and excelling against a top team.

JIM TAYLOR

Vince came in and made a tremendous change by putting Hornung at halfback. And Hornung was the perfect guy for Vince's offense. He could throw, he was a very strong runner, and he was a great blocker. You couldn't play for Vince Lombardi in the backfield unless you could block. That's what Hornung did extremely well.

MAX McGEE

For a running ball club, it's amazing that we caught as many passes as we did because we only threw on pure passing situations where everyone knew you had to throw. Taylor and Hornung were both very fine football players, and they were both very fine pass receivers. They complemented each other; they both blocked for each other. Everyone talks about their running ability, but their blocking ability was of equal note.

GARY KNAFELC

The off tackle play was another key play I ran, Hornung blocking to the weak side. You'd get people in certain formations, and we'd just run at them. Hornung was an excellent blocker.

JIM TAYLOR

Jim Taylor. Green Bay, 1966.

Jim Taylor. Green Bay, 1966.

Well, you didn't even know where Green Bay was. My first contract was $9,500 and a $1,000 bonus, and I was the sixteenth player picked in the whole country in 1958. You didn't know much about the team. They'd just won the two games with Ron Kramer and Hornung the year before, and they only carried a thirty-four-man roster. So you just said, well, you know, and you just go up and go in and do a job and stay focused and work hard and see if you can be a member. I was probably on the verge of being cut a few times, too, right before they kept a full squad. With Scooter McLean in '58 we had a 1-10-1 record. I sat on the different squads, and I didn't do any rushing until the last two games. I gained over 100 yards in both those games, and I said, well, I think maybe I can play this game and be a running back in this league.

JIM TAYLOR

I remember when we had an intersquad game and they finally put me in. We were running goal lines, and Jimmy Taylor was coming. I kind of hit him. Actually, I didn't kind of hit him, I hit him, and made the play.

Vince said, "God damn it! We can't run over that little so-and-so over there?" He said, "Run that play again!"

Well, they ran that play again. And I hit him again.

Vince didn't say anything to me that Saturday, but that Monday he came.

"Well, you keep up the good work and you'll be here a long time," is what he said. And that was the first time he ever said anything to me.

WILLIE WOOD

It's hard to communicate how it was and what it was like back in the late 1950s and when Lombardi came. I could sit down for hours and hours and I don't think we'd be on the same page.

JIM TAYLOR

Jim Taylor, Jerry Kramer, Fuzzy Thurston. Bloomington, Minnesota, 1962.

All teams had some sort of variations, options off the Sweep. It's just a play that we were going to run against everything and be successful. Lombardi would go over and over it at a blackboard for an hour. You really needed to know what everybody was doing. It was a specialization, and you just went over it and over it, and you perfected it. You needed everybody to work together.

No one could figure out how to stop those plays. And once we would line up in a certain formation, we just ran certain plays at you. So you were trying to defense those, because that was it, there wasn't going to be any surprises. We would just defy people and say we're going to block you, we're going to make five, six yards, and we don't care. Bart could check out of it, if he thinks that, but not too many times. They would try to throw the strongest defense up against our sweep formation. It wasn't a guessing game, it was just execution. We just defied people to stop us. We were going to line up in that formation and run it.

JIM TAYLOR

Jerry was an excellent offensive guard. I used to say to people that the difference between Jerry Kramer and Fuzzy Thurston is Fuzzy probably makes more blocks than Jerry, but they ain't as pretty. Jerry used to go out there and he'd just drill somebody, and you'd see the bottoms of the soles of their shoes. They'd be flying through the air and landing on their backs.

KEN BOWMAN

When you talk about the Packers of the '60s, you talk about Lombardi, the championships, the Sweep. The Sweep was Vince Lombardi's pride in motion. It had to work to make our offense work. We were the best at running the Sweep, we knew it would get us yardage and it did. We worked hard to accomplish that goal, and it was accomplished.

Jerry Kramer ran the Sweep to perfection. He was a great athlete. Excellent strength, blessed with great speed and quickness. His mental ability and knowledge of the game were terrific. Jerry excelled in all the phases of the offensive lineman: straight-away power, trap blocking, pass protection, mental attitude. He was an All-Pro guard and should be elected to the Pro Football Hall of Fame.

I always said there are two reasons the Packers were the best. Jerry Kramer is one, and you are looking at the other.

FUZZY THURSTON

Jerry Kramer. Detroit, 1967.

The thing about all that stuff, being there and doing the things we did, and being a part of "The Block," and carrying Lombardi off the field, and, well, who the hell would ever dream that any of this would last more than a few moments? I mean, who would ever dream that twenty-five years later we're still talking about it, that people are still declaring us heroes, that people still remember everything we did? If you can give me one guy on that Green Bay team that felt that this whole thing would last more than a few moments, or a few months, I want to know who it was. Those moments, I guess, were just appreciated, and they captured something for such an incredible number of people, but it just stuns me that it's still talked about.

JERRY KRAMER

Looking back on it now, Jerry had more of a sense of history than the rest of us. He came in there in that last year that Lombardi coached and started at the beginning of the training camp with his little tape recorder. We all rode him a little bit about this. He was chronicling everything going on, and we kind of teased him about it, and he took it good-naturedly. He just had more of sense of history than the rest of us. I mean, the rest of us were just there happy to be playing for a championship team, and there was a natural camaraderie on that team among everybody. Usually you don't have that on a football team. Usually you've got groups and different divisions here and there. There wasn't any of that. Kind of funny in that respect.

KEN BOWMAN

Forrest Gregg. Green Bay, 1966.

I think Lombardi said that Forrest was the most perfect offensive lineman that he had ever seen, and I think he was probably right. He was a whale of an offensive tackle, I'll tell you. Ernie McMillan told me once that if he was going to be blocking Deacon Jones or somebody like that, why, he used to get films of Forrest. He'd want to make sure he got the Green Bay film because he wanted to know how Forrest had blocked the guy. He had a natural ability to do it and make it look easy. He'd come off the ball, and if the ball was going on the inside, he'd be driving off his right foot, hitting the guy with his right shoulder, swinging his left leg around and he had his body between the man he was supposed to be blocking and the ball. And if it was going outside, he'd come off the ball and almost imperceptibly he'd be coming off his left leg, hitting the guy with his left shoulder, swinging that right leg around and he'd be between his man and the ball. He would almost do it effortlessly when you watched it. I don't know if it was by instinct or hard work, but he had perfect technique.

KEN BOWMAN

I liked blocking too. My mentor was Forrest Gregg. He helped me a lot, and we worked together well as a unit. I had to work with both tackles because I switched back and forth, but it was so great working with a guy who had that much muscle, and when I say muscle I mean substance by himself to play ball. And I wanted to be just like him.

MARV FLEMING

Forrest Gregg. Green Bay, 1962.

You know, there was something that was real interesting about playing in Green Bay, and in an odd sort of way a lot of it can be credited to Vernon. In his pictures live the memories of all those great teams and all those great players. And as a present-day player when I was there, I would look at his picture of Forrest Gregg covered in mud, or the Sweep by Jim Taylor or Paul Hornung, or Bart Starr in the pocket, or Vince Lombardi roaming the sidelines, and you could feel that. You could feel that when you stepped on that field because those pictures were so vivid. Ray Nitschke, you could feel his presence when you were on the football field. Granted, they were great players and they won championships. But I think a lot of it was some of the dramatic black and white pictures that Vernon shot in that era.

JAMES LOFTON

Bart Starr. Green Bay, 1964

I think Bart Starr was the most honest quarterback there ever was. He had no favorites. If you were open, you were his favorite. He's not waiting for his favorite guy to come open, come open, come open, and then trying to force the ball to him, like they do now.

MARV FLEMING

Bart had the least athletic ability of all of them but worked harder than any of them. He had the weakest arm, but he worked at it. We used to start in May, he and I. He would throw this weighted football, and I'll never forget this, an old rubber ball, real coarse, with those knobs on it. I think they got it from Voit. And he would throw that to strengthen his arm all the time, and I would catch that ball, just time after time after time. He worked on that constantly to get his arm strength up.

Bart was a great student of the game, studied films all the time. Every night that we were on the road, he and I, we were roommates, we would go over all the different plays. I would tell him, okay, here's the down, here's the distance, here's where we are on the field, what would you call? And he would come up with the play. And we would keep doing this all of the time.

He never got rattled. Great confidence in what he could do. Great confidence in the ball club. And he just didn't make mistakes. He never hurt you.

GARY KNAFELC

Bart was a great help to me my rookie season. He was a veteran, and he took the rookies under his wing. He was trying to instill in us, I think, the sense of tradition that was there and a sense of Packer history and a sense of the pride of the Packers.

MIKE McCOY

Players have got their jobs to do, and they know what they have to do, all they want is to be treated like a man. Bart did that. Bart worked our tails off, basically, but he treated you fairly and no one minded working hard. I've always said that Bart Starr is the nicest, classiest man I've ever met in my life.

LYNN DICKEY

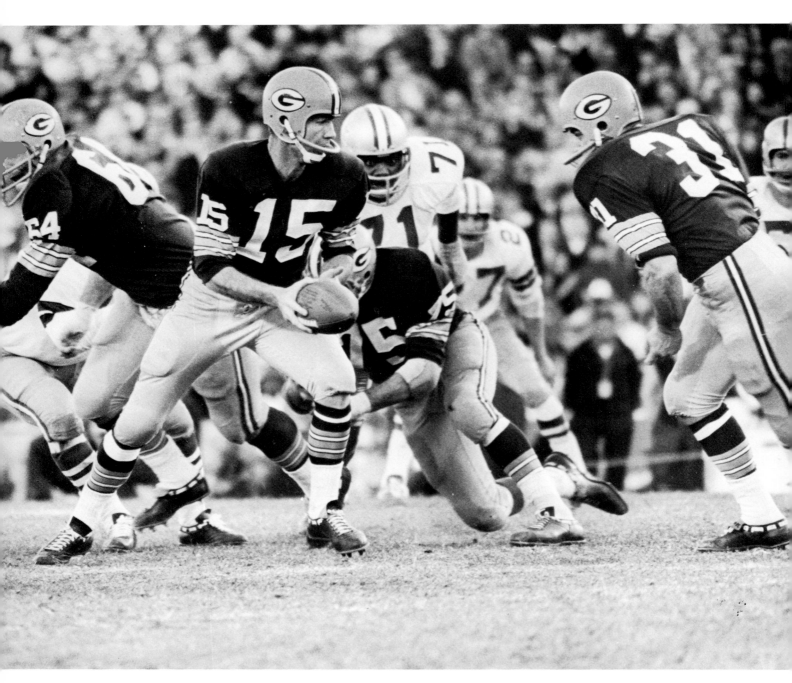

Bart Starr, Jim Taylor. Green Bay, 1967.

Jim Taylor was the best third-down runner I have ever seen play. Paul Hornung, as Lombardi said, was the greatest runner inside of the ten-yard line of all time. Both were very strong, very good at blocking for each other, and together the best two backs to ever play the game on the same team.

FUZZY THURSTON

During the Lombardi era it was natural for pictures of the Packers to be used, and I think other teams noticed that there was a lot of ink coming out of Green Bay, so they started using team photographers themselves. The Lombardi Era brought football into what the game is now in so many ways, including in photography. I had an advantage during those years in the sixties with a gang of excellent football players who knew what they were doing at all times.

VERNON BIEVER

You hear guys talk about how great they were, and they were. I've got a shirt that says, "The older you are, the better you were." But they won championships, and we haven't. We want to have our own legacy, and if we don't, sixty years from now all I'll be telling my grandkids is, "Hey, I met Bart Starr."

BRETT FAVRE

Bart Starr, Vince Lombardi. Green Bay, 1966.

Bart was the perfect quarterback for Lombardi's system. He was an extension of Lombardi on the field, and they worked wonders together. Bart was a very, very smart individual. He never made mental mistakes, ever. He was always well prepared, and he was a very, very intelligent quarterback. And a good arm, a very accurate arm, he doesn't get credit enough for his arm. He was as accurate a passer as there was a passer during those years.

PAUL HORNUNG

Lombardi was in complete charge of the quarterbacks and was in complete charge of the passing game, so he was with Bart all of the time. And Bart knew exactly what Lombardi would do at a certain time, at a certain distance, because they had all these meetings, constantly, as to what to do. Bart listened to him, and eventually he thought like Lombardi.

GARY KNAFELC

It's definitely true that Bart was the on the field an extension of Lombardi. And I think Favre and Holmgren probably have the same kind of relationship. Brett is a little more likely to freestyle it out there than Bart. No reflection on Bart. We were a running team; they are a passing team. But you've got to have that coach-quarterback connection.

MAX McGEE

I think I have a fairly similar working relationship with Brett as Lombardi had with Bart. I would say that Brett tests me more than Bart tested Vince Lombardi. I think Brett is more talented physically. I know that. He has the stronger arm. There's a side to him that believes he can get some things done relying on his physical gifts. I've had some experience with that with Steve Young. It's been my experience, though, that what happens is as a player matures in the position he tends to rely more on his coach.

MIKE HOLMGREN

Bart Starr. Green Bay, 1970.

Bart was a great field general. He didn't have the arm of John Elway, but he was a great general. Bart's biggest asset was his brain. He would take things and store them away and use them at the most opportune moment. Max or Boyd Dowler would say, "I can get this guy to bite on an inside move if you want." And Bart would take that and he wouldn't use it right away. He'd use it when we needed it. Late in his career when his shoulder started going, I don't think he could throw the ball twenty yards, but he was still in there because of his brains, because of what he knew.

KEN BOWMAN

Lamar McHan was the starting quarterback, and he won the first three games for Coach Lombardi. McHan was big, strong. He could throw the ball anywhere you wanted him to. Just a brute of a quarterback. He played an option at Arkansas, so he was a pretty tough kid. Then we went down to play at Pittsburgh.

McHan was a very fine quarterback, but Bobby Layne was the Steelers' quarterback, and we were down in Pittsburgh. Lamar was having a bad day, and at halftime Coach Lombardi made a change and substituted Bart.

Bart did exactly what we had discussed in the halftime meeting with Coach. We had thought that they were in a overshifted zone to the strong side all the time. The safety was responsible for the tight end, and if I could catch a turn-in, with the safety coming in, it could release Dowler, the flanker, for the post. In the first series Bart throws one to me for about fifteen yards, then another one to me for about fifteen yards, and we're down in scoring position. And I said, "Just jack it to me." So he faked it to me, and the safety came up like a shot to get me, and Bart just lobbed it over my head. Dowler caught it and walked the last twenty yards into the end zone, and we won the ball game.

Now, all of this said, Lombardi wasn't the kind of guy who would not have started Mac the next game. He just didn't do those kind of things. He still would have started Mac. But something happened.

At that time we used to all have dinner at a place where all the team used to eat. The coach and his executive committee ate out there too. On the plane ride home Mac had had several beers and was getting out of shape, and by the time the rest of us were out for dinner, he was really out of shape. He came walking in, and I was sitting there and I saw him, so I got up and went to meet him. He and I were together in the All-Star camp and we were the one and two choices of the Cardinals. So I said, "Where are you going, I want to talk to you."

He said, "I'm going to tell that. . . ."

"Now look," I said, "I wouldn't do anything like that. You're drunk, go home, take it easy, and talk to him tomorrow."

"Naw, I'm gonna. . . ." and he went in.

He was traded the next day.

And that's how Bart started to play. He may never have gotten in. Lombardi would have started McHan the next week, no question about it. It would have to take three or four bad games, and McHan hadn't been doing that badly. It was only that we were behind in the Pittsburgh game.

GARY KNAFELC

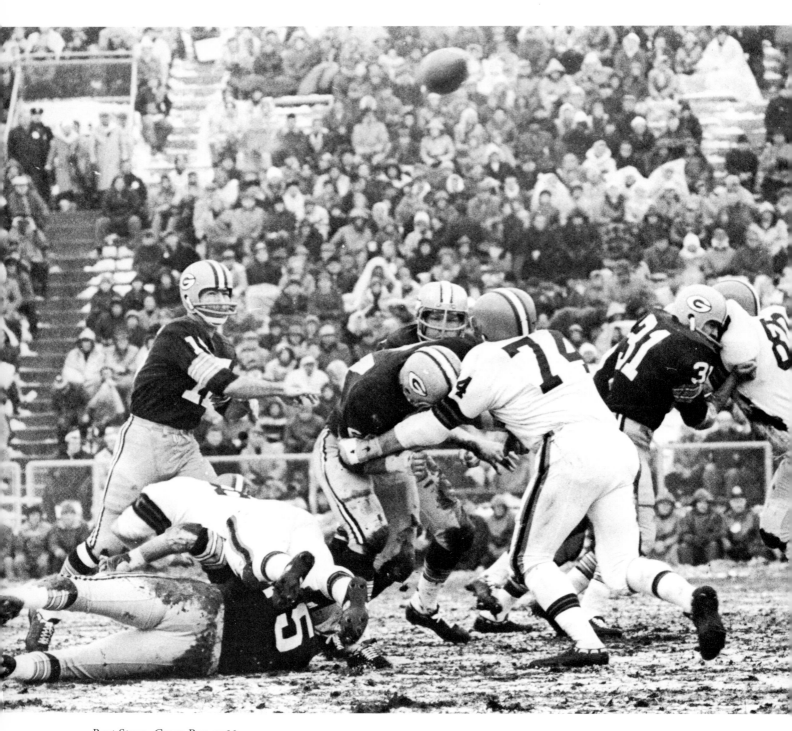

Bart Starr. Green Bay, 1966.

"Honest" is a pretty good characterization of Bart because that was the way Bart played the position, and he was not wrong. He wasn't going to hang you up with the ball. He wasn't going to throw with somebody flying right into your face.

It's a system, a passing game, so to speak. A pattern, not a route. It's the pattern that counts—reading the defense, throwing it to the right guy. It's not that this is Bart throwing to Boyd out here, who runs a twelve-yard out pattern and this is such a wonderful communication that Bart happens to throw the ball to where he catches it before he goes out of bounds. That stuff's elementary. That gets boring.

We used to go out and work in June and July, just the two of us, and by the time training camp rolled around I was sick of running routes on the one-on-one stuff out alone. After a while you could do it blindfolded. When it gets fun is when you put the whole defense out there and you start kind of cutting it apart. And we got to be pretty good at it because we had very intelligent people, and not only throwing the ball and catching it, we had good protection up front. The whole thing worked pretty darn good.

The way we were set up on offense to throw the football, Bart would key the defense and then read where the ball was supposed to go. When he called a play in the huddle, he wasn't necessarily calling the play for an individual, the ball went to the person it should go to based on what coverage was presented. If it was blitz, it was one thing. If it was some sort of man coverage, it was another thing. If it was a rotation one way, the ball would go the other way. He may have had in his mind when he called the play that, well, this play I'd like to get the ball to Carroll, but if the defense wasn't set up that way, he wasn't going to throw it there.

That's one thing we all did very well, we all read defenses, we all knew what the defenses were. You can tell. It got to the point where I could tell coming off the line of scrimmage. I'd see where the defense was going, and then knowing that, sometimes I'd just go ahead and keep running, I didn't even look, and Bart never surprised me. When I coached, I tried to coach the same way. Coming off the line of scrimmage, if you don't know what you're facing by the time you're three or four steps down the field, you're just not paying any attention. If you look at it that way, and you do it all week in practice, and then keep doing it year after year, it's not very difficult.

That's how we functioned, everybody knew what everybody else was doing, and it made it look so simple that it was almost ridiculous. I talked to other players sometimes and they said, "I don't know what you guys are doing. Doesn't look like you're doing anything, but the ball just keeps going down the field."

And I said, "That's the way it's supposed to look. That's the way it's planned."

BOYD DOWLER

Boyd Dowler. Bloomington, Minnesota, 1963

Dowler was like a master. He wanted to do everything perfectly. He wanted to have, like, twenty steps, and make sure he gets that one step there and one step here and come back for the ball.

MARV FLEMING

Boyd Dowler. Dallas, 1967

Max and Boyd were tall and had a different type of running style. They were very different from many of the ends of today. I felt their number one outstanding characteristic was their ability to make the clutch catches under pressure and in crucial situations. They always made the big plays to win the big games.

FUZZY THURSTON

Boyd Dowler and Max McGee were as good a pair of receivers as ever played the game. And two complete opposites. Max was loose as a goose all the time, where Boyd was very intense, very intense. He had great, deceptive speed. Boyd would look like he was going nowhere, and then he was by you.

GARY KNAFELC

If I want to have guys on my team, I want to have guys like Boyd, Max, Carroll, Bob Long. They never showed that individuality thing. They never let individuality get in the way of the team effort.

MARV FLEMING

I had always been a quarterback until I got to Green Bay and Vince made a receiver out of me. I had a lot to learn, but I didn't have a lot to forget, didn't have any bad habits. I was just learning it from the very beginning, and I picked it up pretty quickly. I kind of anticipated the move to end; it didn't surprise me at all. I caught a lot of passes in college, which is kind of strange for a quarterback, but we played a multiple-type offense, half T formation where I was a quarterback, half single wing where I was an eligible receiver. I had never played outside the formation, you know, wide, and I had never been in a three-point stance, but all of that was not that difficult because I could run a little and I could catch all right.

BOYD DOWLER

Max McGee. Los Angeles, 1967.

You know Max is always being characterized as a free spirit and all that kind of stuff, but Max was very disciplined about what he was doing, very disciplined about his football. He wasn't loose about it at all. He was also very, very smart. Carroll Dale certainly was very detail oriented in what he was doing, and his techniques were very sound fundamentally. When you get right down to it, as a group we all were very detail oriented, and we worked with Bart that way. I don't think we'd have been playing, you didn't play for Vince if you were lackadaisical mentally or anything like that. He wouldn't get along with you. That's all there was to it.

BOYD DOWLER

Max knew how to run a pass route, and he knew how to beat players. I remember one time he went up to Lombardi and said, "I have a play for you." Went back in and caught a touchdown. It was because he had a view of the field.

MARV FLEMING

Max was probably the smartest receiver of all of us. He came back to the huddle, and Bart would ask us, you know, "What can you do?" He asked me, I'd say, "I can do anything." But if he talked to Max, he'd say, "It's second and nine and we're on the near hashmark, so I could run a turn-in at twelve and a half."

GARY KNAFELC

To be honest, the first Super Bowl was not as big a deal as it's become, by any stretch of the imagination. I think it's more of a circus now than a football game. I mean, it was a different deal. Nobody knew what was going to happen. We played without a sellout, and we played an unknown factor in how good this team was. We were a dominant team, and they were pretty good. I don't knock that. But at the time I didn't put much significance on it. I was just happy to be there and lucky to have the opportunity to be in the game.

You know, I was pretty dumb because when I caught that first touchdown pass in the history of the Super Bowl I just routinely handed it back to the official, and they routinely kicked it up into the fans and that was the end of that football. If I had any history in mind I would have kept that damn football, which would have been extremely valuable, not for money, but as a prized momento. It's always going to be the first touchdown in the Super Bowl. One time I ran a little ad in the paper out in L.A. to find it, and I got about sixty calls; everybody had an NFL football because I was offering a reward. So I couldn't get it because I had too many offers.

I'm still trying to find that exact picture for that first touchdown. The very first one, where I reached back a caught a quick little post for thirty-seven yards. *Sports Illustrated*'s cover was after I had crossed the goal line. I think they were trying to show that I was kind of straining a little bit, or something. I wanted to find the one where I reached behind me and the ball actually hit my hand and I kind of rolled it up, and I never found that picture. I'm surprised old Vernon didn't get that shot.

As the game got going there, you know, all at once I was catching them right and left. I came over and Hornung said, "You know, you're going to be the MVP of this game." And I says, "Well." That never entered my mind. I wasn't even thinking it, number one. Which I wasn't, by the way, MVP, Bart Starr was. But it was a nice thought.

MAX McGEE

Marv Fleming, Boyd Dowler. Circa 1966.

I was drafted number two in the AFL draft by Denver. It was like a week before, two weeks before, the NFL draft. Green Bay wanted me early in the NFL draft, they said, but Denver had put on the wire that I had signed. I was in Utah. I was at school when they called me. Vince Lombardi called me.

"Marv Fleming?"

"Yes."

"This is Coach Lombardi."

And I says, "Yeah, right. Who is this?"

He didn't say anything, he just handed the phone to the line coach. He says, "Marvin? This is the Green Bay Packers."

I says, "Yes?"

He says, "Have you signed with Denver Broncos?"

"Who's this?"

He says, "I'm a coach with the Green Bay Packers."

And I said, "Who was that on the phone?"

"That was Vince Lombardi."

And I said, "You're kidding me." I didn't know him, I just knew of him. And I said, "Please tell him I'm sorry. I've been getting a lot of different phone calls, please tell him I'm sorry."

"It's on the wire that you signed with Denver."

"I haven't spoken to anybody from the Broncos."

"Well, we're going to draft you right now then."

I said, "Fine. Thank you for calling."

MARV FLEMING

Jim Grabowski. Green Bay, 1967

I remember seeing all these great pictures coming out of Green Bay, and I'd have them up in my office at NFL Films, and we didn't even know who took them. But after a while, you notice his name and you'd start to make the association, and you'd realize, my God, all these great pictures were taken by the same person.

STEVE SABOL

NFL Films

There's a real link with today's team and the teams of the past. Every week at home games, they bring in an honorary captain from the old days, and no matter if he was a ten-year All-Star or a guy who was there for three years, the crowd goes wild.

KEITH JACKSON

We had a ball-possession offense, you see. Our philosophy was we were going to run first and pass second. Today's football is just the opposite. They're not trying to control the line of scrimmage. Only until your Super Bowl teams in the last few years, you had to go back beyond that to the Steelers, who controlled that line of scrimmage. You need two running backs and you need a tight end, you don't need all these wide-outs and all that. Bill Walsh is coming back and he's wanting to instill that with the 49ers again. That one back and all that crap, they can defense that. You cannot be effective with just one running back. You see that Detroit runner, a great runner, Barry Sanders, you can't just run him to win. Run and shoot and all this other crap. You throw second. That's why Bart had great percentages. Everybody in the ballpark didn't know when you were throwing. And we weren't as colorful as Unitas or other teams that throw, throw, throw the ball. But we won. And that was the difference.

JIM TAYLOR

Jim Grabowski and I came up together. We were drafted primarily just to take Taylor and Hornung's place. That was the plan, and it was working. Jimmy was a new breed. It was unfortunate that he tore his knee up in his second year and wasn't able to play to his full potential. He was a 225-pound, 6'2" fullback who had speed, but built big upstairs, he also had power. He had all the talent, could catch the ball in his hands, had good quick feet, could block, could run, tough, he could do it all.

DONNY ANDERSON

Tom Moore. Green Bay, 1963.

I liken the growth of football on television to Arnie Palmer's tremendous popularity in golf. For the first time when golf came in the living room, Arnie was the man. When we first started watching it, he was the man. And maybe, in a way, we were similar there. When football first came into the living room, it was the Green and Gold.

JERRY KRAMER

Television owns everything now. But I guarantee you, the old Lombardi Era is what brought television to the forefront.

MAX McGEE

That type of versatility--where you caught the ball, you blocked, you ran--there's not a lot of guys today who are three-dimensional players. Tom Moore was a good running back.

DONNY ANDERSON

Jerry Kramer, Tom Moore, Fuzzy Thurston, Forrest Gregg. Green Bay, 1961.

There's nothing better than one of those rare pictures, whatever it happens to be, and Vernon's had as many as anybody. You still hit the right moment with that shutter and you've got something that says more than all us announcers can say, I'll tell you that.

MAX MCGEE

Tom Moore came out of Vanderbilt, you know, and me coming out of Tulane, we were in the same conference, and you just kind of automatically grouped together. He was a few years after me. He really had some pretty good talent, you know.

MAX MCGEE

I didn't realize that all of those pictures were Vernon's. It's amazing.

BOYD DOWLER

When I went to Green Bay the offense was really a power game set up by coach Lombardi. There're two philosophies in drafting players for an offense. One is you draft people who have a lot of ability and you build an offense around them. The other philosophy is that you draft individuals who fit into an offense. In Vince Lombardi's case, he drafted people to fit his offense, and it was a power-type game. Running backs split time blocking for each other, providing the key block off a linebacker or middle linebacker. The backs also had a lot of responsibility in the passing game, picking up blitzes. You definitely were involved in the game in that offense.

DONNY ANDERSON

Elijah Pitts. Milwaukee, 1968.

Elijah was a guy who kind of molded into his role being the alternate back. We often felt that he got so good at playing his position that when Pitts came in we didn't lose anything. The efficiency of the team was still there, and the high level of performance was still there. Pitts learned to appreciate that role that he was playing, and he accepted it as such, to the point that he was probably the best substitute back that I had seen in professional football.

WILLIE WOOD

Elijah Pitts still holds the record for the most touchdowns scored in a Super Bowl. Ask Bart Starr about him. He never blew an audible, all the time he played, which you can't say about anybody else. He was very quiet, but Elijah did everything right. You never knew he was there, and suddenly he was in the end zone.

GARY KNAFELC

When you're in high school it's about ninety percent physical and ten percent mental. When you're in college it's about fifty-fifty. Then when you get to the pros it's ninety percent mental and ten percent physical. When you start weighing and measuring and timing and weight-testing guys, the percentage of difference I would say would be less than five percent. But the difference is the mental aspect of it.

PAUL COFFMAN

Pittsy played nine years, a great person to be with. You didn't have to play an ego game with him. He went in, he did his job, he had good feet, he could move, he could catch the ball pretty well, and he didn't make mistakes. That's why Lombardi liked him: he didn't make mistakes. Pitts and Garbo and I kind of carried the mail most of that second Super Bowl year.

DONNY ANDERSON

Hank Gremminger, Green Bay, 1963.

Football is the ultimate team sport. You've got eleven defense, eleven offense, and basically you've got to get everybody going in the same direction. There are so many things in football that you can relate to life. Just the ups and downs. Overcoming things not being fair, overcoming adversity. These are things you meet in life. You can look at a lot of football players who have been successful in life, and they can basically trace it back to the habits that they had playing football.

PAUL COFFMAN

You had good football players and you executed. You came to play each down, every down, and you only played twelve or fourteen games. You had good football players on both sides of the ball and, I don't know, we felt that we really had a nucleus of a very good football team in '61 and '62. We competed against all the other teams and were successful. You can go back but you really can't take the teams out of context. We just had good football players. But I do think they were as good as any football players today. Without a doubt.

JIM TAYLOR

Dave Robinson. Green Bay, 1964.

Training camp? Blood, sweat, and tears. Vince Lombardi and training camp are synonymous to me. There's nothing like a Vince Lombardi training camp, I tell you, nothing like it at all. I was never in the military, but if boot camp was half as bad as a Vince Lombardi training camp then, I tell you what, anybody that comes through boot camp should be saluted. It was tough.

One year, I wanted to get a raise, a big raise from Vince, so before training camp I worked out. I used to run three miles every morning, three miles every afternoon, and in between I used to run wind sprints, in my football shoes, wind sprints so I'd be ready for it, right? I went to camp at 233, I normally played at 236, 37, 38, right in that area. I was in great shape. And the first week, I'd have liked to die. It killed me. You just could not get ready for training camp. I remember Vince saying so many times, he said that we're going to make it so hard, so hard here in training camp that come the fourth quarter in a big game is going to be easy. And he did, and it was. We won a lot of games in the fourth quarter, so he must have known what he was talking about.

DAVE ROBINSON

The first training camp with Lombardi, naturally, was the toughest of all of them. Or maybe we just got used to them after that, I don't know.

See, what you would do, you'd come out to warm up. Coach Lombardi was in charge of the offense, that was his baby. Not only the running plays but, in particular, the passing game. So he would have all the receivers and the quarterbacks out early and we would go through our warm ups and actually run the patterns and everything prior to practice. Then he would call everybody together and do the up-down drills and all that, calisthenics, and he would kill us with that, just kill us. We did the whole workout, and then you would take a lap, and then you would start the passing, just a warm up passing game, and then come back with seven-on-sevens, and then maybe a little scrimmage, and then you'd run wind sprints. And then you'd go in. Twice a day. I was down to 212 pounds. I just could not gain any weight at all. All the guys were just dying. Hawg Hanner was in the hospital twice. That's the only thing that kept me going, because Hawg would be in the up-downs behind me, and if I thought I was going to die, I looked back and saw Hawg and I'd think if Hawg can do it, I can do it. But all the sudden he'd turn real red and pass out. Pick him up, take him to the hospital.

At that time they believed in all kinds of crazy stuff. We could not have water on the practice field. Sure. You couldn't even have ice. That's why I had so many pulls and all that stuff, see. It was asinine. You sweat, you've got to replace it. It's nothing to do with science, it's just common sense. But they wouldn't let you. In fact, Bart and I would do a thing, I'd ask him to throw me an out so I could dive for the ball and I would miss it, but I'd hit the ground by the ice bucket. They had it out there in case you had injuries. So you'd reach in and grab a handful of ice and bring it back and share it with all of the guys. We had that little thing going.

GARY KNAFELC

Willie Davis, Ron Kostelnick. Green Bay, 1965.

Let me tell you about Willie Davis. When I saw him the first time, he walked into training camp as a well-established All-Pro, and I was in awe of him. And then after getting to know him a little bit, I just had great, great respect for him. And then after playing (when Dan Curry got traded and I became the starting left linebacker and I played next to Willie) the respect just turned into admiration.

The primary asset he had was his mind. You could never run the same play twice on Willie Davis. If it was successful, even when it wasn't successful, you could never run the same play twice. If he had never seen the play before, he'd have the same results. If you only tried to run it one time and had moderate success, the next time look for a loss. He was that good.

I guess the greatest thing I can say about Willie Davis is that when I went to Washington George Allen brought me in and he was showing me some of his scouting films of Green Bay and he had isolations of Willie and me playing the defense and he says, "What are you and Willie playing here?" And I told him the defense, and he said "Well how come on the other side Lionel and Lee Roy are playing it different?" And I told him, well, that's just how Willie Davis was. Willie had strengths. And I had strengths. Willie made sure I played my strengths and he played his strengths. And no matter what the defense called for, he said we're playing it this way and covered all the positions. And we were hard to scout against, according to George Allen. That's how Willie was. Extremely intelligent defensive end.

You may have guessed I just have a great deal of admiration for Willie Davis. But I'll tell you one thing about Willie. Willie Davis did not want the end to downblock on his legs. Willie Davis has little legs. Little teeny legs. In fact, a couple guys said he had a job during the off seasons stamping holes in doughnuts. He told me when I came in, when I took over left linebacker, and I told you I have a great deal of respect for Willie Davis, he said, "I don't care what you do, don't let the tight end come down on me." He says, "You keep him off of me and I'll roll to the outside and I'll take your position" —which would be the nine hole— "and you just take mine"—which is the seven. And that's how we played it. When the tight end went down, I rode him down and kept him off of Willie. When Willie felt the pressure, he would drop and pivot and roll to the outside, and any wide plays which would normally be the linebacker's, Willie took them. Any off-tackle plays became mine. We did it for years; it worked out very very well. We just exchanged positions. . . . I tried to explain it to other defensive ends, and no one could grasp it. They all could get the concept of me keeping the end off of them, but they couldn't get the concept of protecting me. I'd get mob-blocked.

I played with a lot of defensive ends. I played with Deacon Jones, I played with Ron McDole. I played with bigger men, I played with stronger men, I played with faster men, I went to the Pro Bowl and played with different defensive ends there, I played with Hall of Famers. But there was nobody, nobody was as good a defensive end as Willie Davis. No one came close to Willie Davis.

DAVE ROBINSON

The way I used to respond to that was: "When have you seen a racehorse with big legs?"

WILLIE DAVIS

Henry Jordan, Willie Davis. Green Bay, 1965.

Henry Jordan had a playing style much like mine. Interesting that the two of us came from Cleveland. We played a year at Cleveland together. Jordan had the good quickness as an inside rusher, but he very seldom overpowered someone. He would just kind of slither through a crack or, almost off a movement of quickness, he was able to penetrate. He was very slender, and he could take a seam and split two offensive linemen. You talk about how my legs are built, Henry was just the opposite. He had very big and strong legs, and I think once he was able to split two guys, he was just able to really power his way between them. It was Henry Jordan's strongest asset that once the linemen allowed him to get in the seam, he had enough strength and enough quickness to get up inside before they could really regroup on him.

WILLIE DAVIS

Willie Davis would pick up everything, without a doubt. Willie was a very intelligent guy, as were most of the guys who played with us. You know, I always say that Vince was bright in putting his talent together because not only did he bring talented guys in there, the guys were pretty smart. There was always a way of making an adjustment to make sure you don't get beat the second time in a play, and Willie, of course, being one of our veterans at the time, would always pick up on that. If we happened to do something that would break down and they were able to make a big run against us, the next time he would adjust to it. And that was the strength of our defense.

WILLIE WOOD

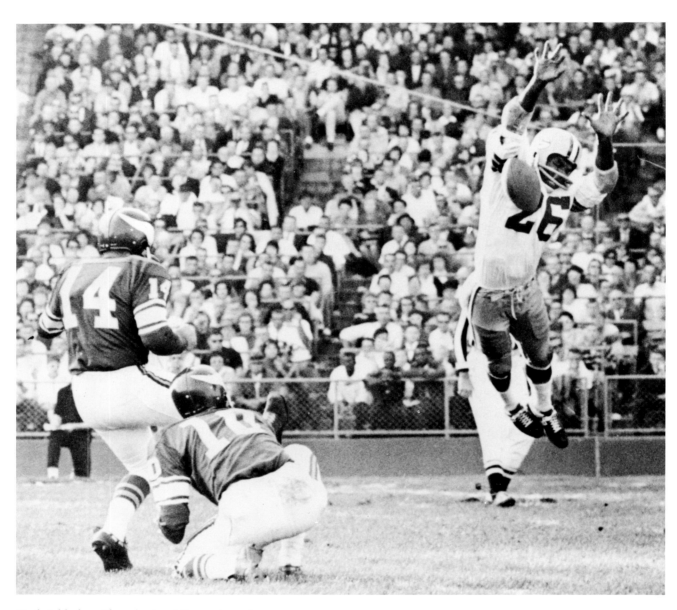

Herb Adderley. Bloomington, Minnesota, 1963.

Our philosophy on defense in reference to the passing game was funnel everything to me. My job was to take care of anything that came inside. If we got beat outside, that was your fault. If we got beat inside, it was mine. That's the way we played. All the guys we had back there, I'm speaking of Adderly, Jeter, Tom Brown, and myself.

Herb was probably the most talented one of us all in terms of just natural athletic skills. Herb had speed, quickness, and agility, and he was just a great natural athlete. I didn't have any speed close to the kind of speed that Herb had. He could run as fast as he needed to run.

As a group we just worked together, and those things that we felt we may be vulnerable in, it was always maybe just the strength of somebody else, and we just played with that. We had the ability in our defense to conjure our defense to a point where we were playing somebody else's strength, and it worked out for us.

WILLIE WOOD

I met Willie Wood and Herb Adderly after I came in. It's always going to be a part of the tradition of the past, I mean, because those guys were great players, and they played on some of the best teams that were ever up there. Those guys are legends, they fulfilled everything, the top of the profession, they won Super Bowls, they did great things. To me, when you hear those names, you think of success.

MARK MURPHY

Herb Adderley, Elijah Pitts, Willie Wood. Milwaukee, 1963.

Actually, there were only about four teams that I thought would be interested in looking at a guy like myself. There was the New York Giants, and, I think it was Cleveland, the 49ers, and Green Bay. But as soon as I wrote the letter to Green Bay, they responded right back, and I didn't send out the other letters. I never knew what the other teams' responses were because I took it on a first-come first-served basis. Green Bay was going through a transition. Vince had just come on board there. I was looking for those teams that looked like they might need help. And, of course, Green Bay was just perfect for that. I guess maybe a week after I sent the letter to Green Bay they responded. They were on their way out to play they Rams, making their west coast trip, and they told me to hold off from signing with anybody, they'd be out and they'd talk with me.

Jack Vainisi, the assistant general manager at the time, contacted me and invited me over to the hotel, and so I went over to the hotel and visited with them and talked with Coach Lombardi for a moment. He was very cordial. I didn't get a feel of the tough man image at the time. As a result of it, my impression was that the coach is a very nice man. Now, of course, Jack Vainisi himself is a very nice man, but Jack was always the same all of the time. Vince, you know, put on different faces based upon what the situations were.

They told me that they were interested and they asked me not to sign with anybody and when they got back to Green Bay they were going to send me a contract. No negotiation, they just gave me a contract. And I don't mind telling you it was only about $6,500—at that time, all the money in the world. Just an opportunity to go to camp and try to make a team was what I had set out to do, and I was very pleased.

I always tell people it was just luck. I was just at the right place at the right time, and they were interested in taking a look at people. Because they needed help at the position, they could afford to sit around and wait for you to come along in camp. Teams who knew who their players were going to be, they started letting you go right away. So I was just fortunate in that sense.

My rookie season we were in the championship game. Second year and third year we won it. My second year I started playing regular.

WILLIE WOOD

Willie Wood was the consummate pro. He was just a force, one of those guys you respected. You looked up to what he'd done in his career.

MIKE McCOY

Dave Hampton. Cleveland, 1969.

A good football game is much like a stage play that reaches a climax. Vernon Biever has always had the ability to recognize the drama of the situation. He knows the denouement of the game and where that point is coming in a contest, and he's always been poised and ready to take that picture when it comes along. His strength is anticipation, but that's just knowledge of the game. It's the recognition of the human emotion of the event that comes through in Vernon's work.

JIM IRWIN
WTMJ Radio

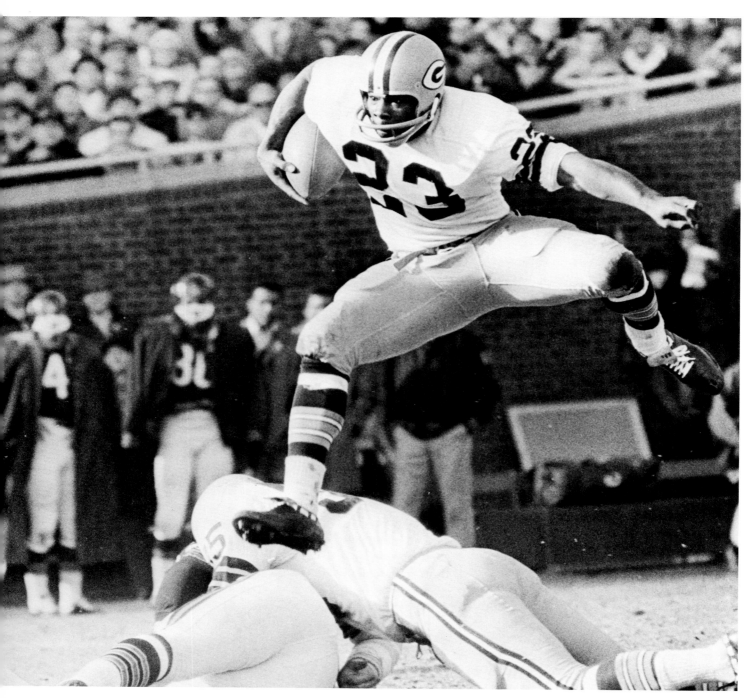

Travis Williams. Chicago, 1967.

What a great talent. He was the greatest kickoff returner that I or anybody else had ever seen. He was a talent.

MAX McGEE

Travis had the speed. He had everything to go with it. He had the size, certainly. Nobody really knew how fast he was because he would only run as fast as he had to run. You talk about running those slant plays, he was maybe the best running back I've seen on slants during the years that I was in professional football. He could time the way he hit that hole in such a way that the linebackers never had a chance. Because he could put on that second burst of speed, he'd just blow right past them.

We got to the point where we said here's this guy with all this kind of speed, how can we utilize it, and then decided to try to put him back on kickoffs, and that's where he found his place. He got to be the man in running those kickoffs back. He learned to time that to a point where he could just eat you up. The guy was a work of art, to watch him run those kickoffs back.

We dubbed him "The Roadrunner." I remember we went up to Pittsburgh one year and we felt we could beat them fairly easily, but they gave us a tough time. And everytime they would score against us, they would kick off, and Travis would run the damn thing back. We were on the field the whole day. After the game, all the guys from the Steelers come up and said, "Man, where you all get this guy from?"

We said, "The Roadrunner? He's one of those cartoon characters."

WILLIE WOOD

Donny Anderson. Green Bay, 1968.

Donny was a good back, no question about it. The man was smart, he could catch the ball, he knew everything about the position.

JOHN BROCKINGTON

Donny was a good guy and a great player. I kind of got criticized a little bit in my rookie year, and he'd come up and say, "Don't worry about it, they did it to me too, it'll all work out."

MIKE McCOY

At the start of the last drive in the Ice Bowl there was never the doubt that we wouldn't score. I still remember that like it was yesterday. In the huddle there was never any conversation except about getting it done. Get it done. That was what made the Packers the great team that they were.

DONNY ANDERSON

Ray Nitschke. Green Bay, 1966.

I was a reserve. I met the team when they were in the exhibition season in North Carolina. The first thing I was told by the equipment manager was that this guy, Lombardi, is really tough and I had better behave myself or I won't be around.

RAY NITSCHKE

Coming in my rookie year, I'd heard of Ray Nitschke but I'd never really seen him, you know. I was in college when the Packers won those first Super Bowls, and a high school senior, and you couldn't really see the guys when they were wearing their helmets and they didn't have the sideline television cameras. So I meet Ray Nitschke, and here's a guy who's got horn-rimmed glasses, I think they were brown, bald, very little upper body, skinny legs, and no teeth. But his hands were huge and he had tremendous forearms. I said, "This is Ray Nitshcke? You've got to be kidding me." Then I saw him play, right next to him all the time, and his work ethic and how he hustled.

Ray was very friendly to the rookies, but when I got into my first preseason game, they break the huddle and we come out, and Ray's standing behind me and he starts yelling at me.

He says, "Hey rookie! Watch the pass! Watch the run! Watch the draw!"

They snap the ball, and it was a draw.

After the play he comes up to me, he says, "I told you what they were going to do."

I said, "Well, Ray, you gave me three choices, and I took A."

MIKE McCOY

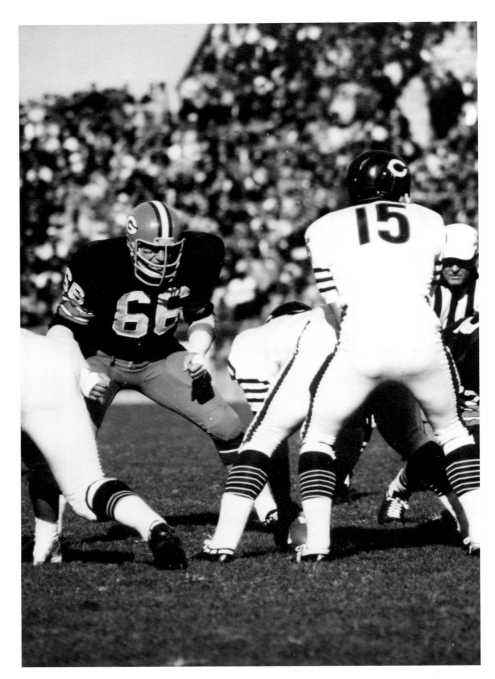

Ray Nitschke. Green Bay, 1967.

Pound for pound there's never been a linebacker that's come close to Ray Nitschke. Dick Butkus, everybody says was the greatest linebacker, but the truth of the matter is that when Dick Butkus came into the league, and if you asked Dick he'd probably tell you the same thing, he stunk up the joint. And George Halas gave Dick Butkus—this is what I heard, I don't know if it's true or not, but I believe it is—gave him a film, a high-light film of Ray Nitschke. Told him to take it home after his rookie year and said, "You study this on the off-season, and when you come back I want you to play just like this. And you could see then a lot of the things he did he copied from Ray Nitschke. The only thing to make a case for Dick Butkus versus Nitschke, Butkus weighed 250, Nitschke barely weighed 230 soaking wet. But still, pound for pound, I tell you, he could hit you like you can't believe.

And Ray was extremely intelligent. He talked a lot of talk and yak, but he was an extremely intelligent player. If Ray had one weakness it was covering a fast back out of the backfield. In fact, in the championship game in '65 against the Browns, they had a play, they opened up the game with the play, and the play was to put Jimmy Brown one-on-one with Ray. And when Jimmy came down he veered to the other side to run away from Ray, but Ray talked to me. In fact, if you look at the play, the opening play of the championship game in '65, when Jimmy caught the ball, I'm down there, Ray's down there, we helped each other. Ray was a talker. You never had to guess where Ray was, he was always going to tell you.

"I'm inside Robbie! Get outside!"

He talked the whole game. I tell you, he never shut up. Sometimes he overtalked. Like one time I remember, we picked up the check-off from Munson in Detroit. They had the same numbering system we did, so if he checked off to a sixty-seven, it was the same sixty-seven we had. It was the seven hole, that was my play. And so we knew it. Everybody knew it and we listened to hear it. So Munson comes out and—he had a live color, we picked up his live code—so he calls his live color for sixty-seven, and then Ray . . .

"Robbie! They're coming your way! They're coming your way Robbie!"

And Munson stopped. And looked. So he knew we knew now. He had to run the play, and we stopped it, but the next time he came out they had a new color, and we never figured it out. We knew the plays, but they had new colors. He came back and used the old colors just to mess with us and didn't run it. Ray overtalked that time. But that was one of his strengths: if Ray knew something was coming, he let you know. He was a real general out there, he was the man. Ray was the man out there, he was.

DAVE ROBINSON

Nitschke always had that ability, as well as most of the other guys, of getting up for the big ball game. Of course, you know Ray being a Chicago boy, he always liked to beat the Bears. He's going home, he's going to show his wares. He always excelled against them, always played well against the Bears.

WILLIE WOOD

Ray Nitschke. Green Bay, 1971.

In practice I went against Nitschke. It's true that he approached practices, essentially, like he was approaching games. Ray took the position that he had a reputation to uphold, so he'd go out on the field and whether he had a helmet on or not, you'd better have your eyes open because Ray was just liable to try to make you eat a bone. He was certainly tough. Lombardi used to have this great big tower that he'd climb up and he'd watch practice from. Well, one day the doggone thing, the wind came up and the tower, it was one of these steel rod towers, and the damn thing started toppling, and it came over and it hit Ray right on the top of the helmet and, in fact, drove one of the bolts right through the plastic on his helmet and knocked him to the ground. It could have been a bad situation. He got up and said, "Whoa, wait a minute," and walked away.

KEN BOWMAN

Ray Nitschke. Los Angeles, 1967.

As much as everyone believes that you got to be able to run the football to win, I don't think that that's necessarily the case. I think the ability to stop the run is much more important.

Brian Noble

I felt, and I think any successful set of linebackers probably feels the same way, that we were the best blend, the best trio of linebackers that ever came into the game. And the thing is, other people probably think that, and all I can say is the proof of the pudding is in the tasting.

Daryl Lamonica was a friend of mine; we came up the same year and played an All-Star game together. In Super Bowl II he told me the thing that shocked him. They came in, the Oakland Raiders, doing real well, and Daryl said the thing that got him was he couldn't believe that linebackers could get so deep on a pass. Lee Roy and myself, we used to get fifteen, twenty yards back on passes. And yet, when he tried to run little flare passes underneath, we got up and covered them. Outside linebackers today, they take after the Lawrence Taylor school. All they want are sacks, where we had interceptions. We also gave underneath coverage to the corners.

Dave Robinson

All our linebackers had mobility. They all had strength and speed and the quickness that is required for a linebacker. Dave Robinson and Lee Roy Caffey were very big for linebackers at that time. Ray Nitschke was more of the kind of guy you might see out there today. Ray only weighed about 215 or 220 pounds. But they all had speed and great quickness, and most importantly, they were all tremendously fine athletes. Of course, Lee Roy, you know, he ran track in college, and Dave was a basketball player. So was Nitschke. Those guys had all kinds of athletic skills. I suspect they would have excelled at any position you might have put them at. They had that kind of ability.

Willie Wood

Lee Roy Caffey. Green Bay, 1967.

You're just an object, and they're just using you. You're just a piece of meat.

JIM TAYLOR

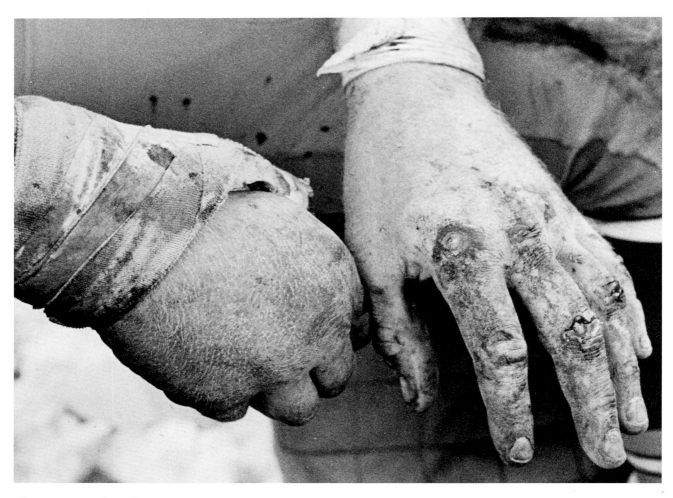

Ken Bowman. Green Bay, 1966.

Kenny Bowman was from the Lombardi Era. I think Lombardi drafted him. And Kenny was always amazing to me because, you know, he wasn't the biggest guy, but he was very sound, very aggressive, and always fired up. He had those pale blue eyes, and he was a bleeder, man. He was like the Bayonne Bleeder, you know what I mean. And he loved it. His face would become red, and you could see those cold blue eyes staring up from behind that red. He was all fired up and breathing hard. He loved it, man. He was a great competitor, Kenny Bowman, a stand-up dude.

JOHN BROCKINGTON

They called Ken Bowman Frankenstein. Big solid forehead, long hair, and this brace with chains from his arm to his shoulder. His shoulder was really bad, so he had a chain attached to a piece of material wrapped around his bicep, and it was hooked onto his shoulder pad so his arm wouldn't go above ninety degrees, limiting the range of motion. He was quite an activist, you know, on a lot of things. Here's another guy who worked really hard. Obviously he did, to get his law degree while he was playing. He was great.

MIKE McCOY

It's my left hand, because the right hand that year, I had broken my thumb. I didn't realize that I had broken my hand. My wife and I went out to eat afterwards, and I kept dropping the fork, and I told her maybe I'd better go over to the hospital. And they shot it and they said it was busted, and then they put it in a little minicast, you know, like a plaster cast and taped it up. Anyway, this was a couple weeks later, and I still had the partial cast on my right hand, so I was not really that interested in trying to keep them away from me with my right hand, so I had my left hand doing double duty. Usually centers, you can bend your wrist in such a fashion that you can use the palm of your hand to push off and get back, but the doggone busted right hand made me basically do everything with the left hand, and that's why the left hand got eaten up the way it did. You inevitably hit somebody in the shoulder pads or the face mask and rip some skin off. It should have been in color.

KEN BOWMAN

John Brockington. Milwaukee, 1971.

Brock came in '71. John Brockington, when I first saw the kid I said, "Wow." Great ballplayer. He had a great physique. Looked like he was just chisled out of steel. He had a great attitude and could run the ball. He was unstoppable. We called him "The Brockington Horse." He was just wild.

DAVE ROBINSON

I don't regret anything. I had a good time. I had some good years.

JOHN BROCKINGTON

Brock was this super, super, fullback. Like Grabowski he had upper body fullback strength, but lower body running back legs. I have fond memories of 1971. The deal back then was that tandem backs were important to the offensive game plan. I had had a really good season the prior year and then Brock came in, and he and I set the record for the most yards as a tandem offense in the NFL ever, at that time. He had like 1,100 yards (I don't remember exactly how many he rushed--over a thousand), and I had 700-and-something, plus over 300 in pass receiving, plus his, for over 2,200 yards total offense. Brock was a great guy and a great runner.

DONNY ANDERSON

John Brockington. Milwaukee, 1972.

A great athlete. We had a lot of young guys coming in, but John was our ace, so to speak. I knew that he was going to do well, and I suspected that with him at that position we weren't going to lose very much. Brockington had the same stuff that Jimmy Taylor had. Perhaps foot speed, maybe he was just a little faster than Jim. Just as mean and just as ornery, you understand, as a runner, and just as big. Running down a field with two men in his way, he would run over them. He was a load too. I'm glad that I wasn't one of the two men.

WILLIE WOOD

It was just a natural gait for me. I guess somewhere in high school somebody said you were supposed to run with your knees up or something like that. I don't know, I read one of these books. But then it became a natural gait for me. There's a couple of running backs now that run the same way. And, you know, everybody's different. O.J. Simpson had that long stride, kind of a low, long stride, and Larry Csonka, he ran his way, and Floyd Little ran one way, and I had high knee action. And it served me well.

JOHN BROCKINGTON

John Brockington. Chicago, 1971.

Nineteen seventy-two was a good year for us. Everything was working. It's funny, because '71 was so bad, and '72 we came in and we were kicking booty, man, it was like, holy smoke, what's going on here? I can tell you what happened. Number one, we got Mac Lane. And we got Chester Marcol. The year before we lost three different games by a field goal or less—one of them three to nothing against the Minnesota Vikings—and had two ties. And Chester comes in his rookie year and leads the league in scoring, kicking the ball from all over the place. And we got Willie Buchanon. We used to get beat on the deep pass, and when Willie came, Al Matthews moved to strong safety, and Willie stopped that. We had Willie and Ken Ellis on the corners, two all-pro cornerbacks right there, and that foolishness stopped. And all the sudden, boom. We started winning football games. That's what happened in '72.

John Brockington

In 1972 I think we were 6-5 at one point or 5-6. We went undefeated the rest of the year. We beat Minnesota; we won the division. But then we went down to play Washington, and they beat us. We had the better team. That was the year that Larry Brown was MVP of the league. We figured, hold them to twenty points. They scored sixteen. But everybody knows what happened that day.

Dave Robinson

Those were some good guys, boy. Those were some good days.

John Brockington

We had a potent running attack, Brockington and MacArthur Lane, and a good offensive line in front of them. We just more or less ran through the central division. Brockington had a thousand yards rushing every year that I was there. And MacArthur Lane on the weak side is a mismatch no matter how you call it. I'd put my money on MacArthur Lane any time if I can get him the ball on the weak side against a weak-side safety or a weak-side halfback.

KEN BOWMAN

In Brockington's first years, he looked like he was just waiting for MacArthur Lane to come to the team. And then when he and MacArthur Lane were in there together it was awesome. Great tandem. Both of them blocked well, great blockers. MacArthur Lane was a well-above-average runner, and Brockington was a great runner. So now no matter which way we come, no matter who's got the ball, you've got to contend with a blocker and a runner. They carried the game. They ran a sweep very effectively. They both had good speed. Neither of them were speedsters, but they had enough speed to get to the outside.

DAVE ROBINSON

Mac, boy, he was tough. And he was aggressive. He was just hard, man, he was hard. He wouldn't let down. He was a fireball and a hardhead, boy. And could he block. Oh man, he could uproot people. He would uproot you, man, like I never saw a running back do. Art Malone was good, but Mac, he could get a linebacker and tag him, man. Oh my goodness. Mac was great.

JOHN BROCKINGTON

I still haven't seen an overall athlete as good as MacArthur Lane. He could kick, he could pass, he could catch, he could run. I think that he was one of the finest athletes that I have ever seen. And could he block. My, my, my.

CHESTER MARCOL

*Scott Hunter, MacArthur Lane,
John Brockington. Green Bay, 1973.*

Chester Marcol. Green Bay, 1973.

I was just like any other college kid, dreaming of being able to do something special throughout my career, you know, but a lot of these things happened quick. Of course, it was beyond my expectations.

There were still some guys who had played in the Super Bowls. Dave Robinson, Ray Nitschke, Ken Bowman, Gale Gillingham. But to be very honest with you, I never thought about it. That was the thing that I really like about that team, was that there was some kind of closeness there. Even though we had a ton of young kids on that team, there was no break between the veterans and the new guys, there was no animosity, no such thing as, you know, "You're a bum because you're a rookie," and all that. I didn't see that. After the training camp. Rookies take a ribbing every rookie camp, that's just a part of life in football, but I didn't see that at all after the season started.

That's what I enjoyed. Like, the daily routine. We were watching films, and then we had lunch before we went out to practice, I remember like five, six of us got together and each week a different guy would go get lunch meat, you know. I was sitting around with Ken Bowman and Tommy Joe Crutcher and Dave Robinson and a few other guys and we just kind of pooled together, had good conversation and not necessarily always something about football. These little small things like that, they make a big difference. I felt something real close there, something special.

CHESTER MARCOL

Chester was different for a kicker. Because most kickers, you know, as a rule, well, they don't have much personality. Chester did. Chester was a kick. He comes into Green Bay, a young kid out of college, and he's hanging out with everybody on the team, he didn't just go and disappear after practice, he'd stick around with the team and have a good time. Just a real nice guy with a great attitude. But the thing is, he could kick, man! The guy could kick. And he was tough, mentally tough, too. He loved being on the team and he was instantly adored because he could kick the ball through the uprights from thirty, forty yards out consistently. It was what we needed, boy. We loved Chester.

JOHN BROCKINGTON

In my career, probably the number one thing, by far, that I'm identified with is that touchdown I scored against the Bears. If I'm not mistaken, I think it was voted the fourth most exciting play in the Green Bay history. I just went and donated that touchdown football to the Packer Hall of Fame last March when John Anderson and Lee Remmel were inducted. I had to battle my wife for a year before she would agree with me.

CHESTER MARCOL

Scott Hunter. Milwaukee, 1972.

Scott Hunter was solid, he was smart, and he worked hard. And he could certainly throw the ball farther than Billy Kilmer could throw. How strong was Joe Montana's arm? How strong was Fran Tarkenton's arm? Scott had as strong an arm as Fran Tarkenton in those days. I mean, Tarkenton threw those little looping passes, you know? Those teams all knew to just keep it in their quarterback's range. Scott played gallantly.

JOHN BROCKINGTON

I don't think Scott Hunter got his due. He produced when it counted.

CHESTER MARCOL

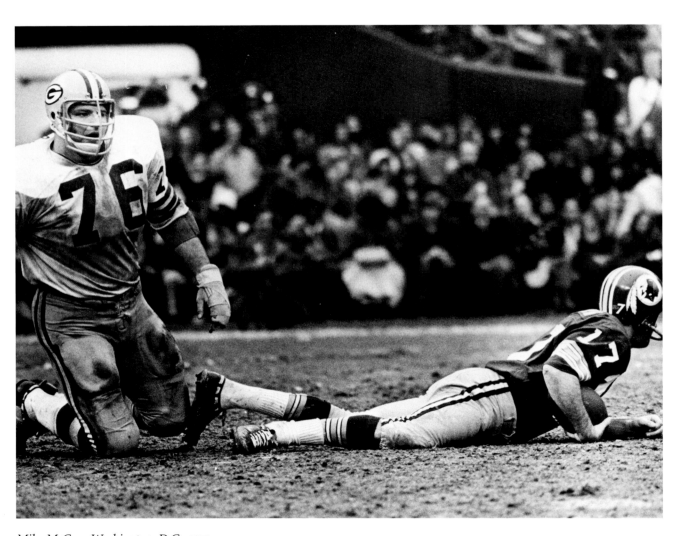

Mike McCoy. Washington, D.C., 1972.

Mike McCoy was solid. He was the kind of guy who would really get fired up, keyed up for football games. And he was a big load. Mike must have weighed, in those days, 280, really big. Linemen got to weigh 300 pounds when I was playing, but there wasn't a lineman who weighed 300 pounds when I started. Michael was real strong against the run, real strong. A very solid guy. You could always count on Mike. He was not going to make mistakes, he was not going to hurt you. He's going to give you the best that he had, always. He was tough.

JOHN BROCKINGTON

Mike McCoy was actually one of the guys, to be honest with you, that I looked up to. There was something special about him, because of his way of life. You know, no craziness, no partying, and all that stuff. As time went on, if somebody would ask me the question, who were the guys that I really respected in the long run, I think Mike McCoy would be in my top few people.

CHESTER MARCOL

My first game was a night game. It was hot and muggy, air wasn't moving very much. I had just come up from the College All-Star game, and I was just literally scared. Here you were, going from college football, even though I played at Notre Dame, to pros, and you don't know how things are going to work out and you just want to give it your best shot. And you just got a real taste of what pro football was like, getting beaten by the Kansas City Chiefs who had just come off of winning the Super Bowl after the 1969 season.

There were a lot of changes going on. I had just gotten married. We were married July 4, it was ninety-five degrees. Our recessional hymn was Battle Hymn of the Republic. I went right from there to Chicago, and three days later I'm playing the College All-Star game. And then Al Matthews and I drive up together to Green Bay and meet my wife. She was already in Green Bay, and got the apartment. I didn't even see the apartment until late August, didn't even live with my wife yet because I was in training camp. Al Matthews and I were roommates our rookie year. And little did we realize, we were the integrated couple. That was the first time, I think, that that had ever happened in Green Bay. We were just rookies, we didn't know any different. We're great friends even today.

MIKE McCoy

Philadelphia, 1974.

In the Packers' lean years, it's almost that the team did not live up to Vernon.

STEVE SABOL
NFL Films

Vernon is consistent in his work, diligent. That's obvious in how he continued to turn out outstanding photos when the team wasn't of the Lombardi-Era caliber. Now the national focus is coming back to Green Bay, and Vernon is still an outstanding photographer. He doesn't have the field to himself as much as he had at one time; the number of people who are covering teams has just grown enormously, far more than we've had since the sixties. But Vernon will still be an outstanding photographer in that field, with that many more competitors working on the same subject.

JIM IRWIN
WTMJ Radio

Mark Koncar. Green Bay, 1978.

Anybody can do it in practice or preseason, but when you start playing sixteen games, year after year, that's when you really appreciate the mental toughness.

I saw guys from major colleges come up to Green Bay, guys that won national championships and had year after year of winning, and when we were 3-10 and it was December and it was minus-ten degrees, all the sudden these people weren't really wanting to play. And I was thinking, you don't play because you win or because you lose, you play because you love the game. If it's three degrees or if it's ninety-three degrees, if you love it you're still going to be out there.

Paul Coffman

If you are a football enthusiast and you love the game, the Green Bay Packers *are* football.

Sean Jones

This is what the NFL should be about. If a person is really and truly a pro football fan, it would be incumbent upon him to come here and attend a game and just witness what occurs here.

Ron Wolf

Everybody lives and dies for the Packers. There's no tradition like it. I love it here.

Mark Chmura

Green Bay was the best place to play, I mean the best. The loyalty that they have. Late in the year you could be 0-14 or 14-0, it doesn't matter, there's going to be 50,000 people there. There's no other place like that. Anywhere else, you come in there 0-14, there's just no way. There are so many fair-weather clubs. But in Green Bay it's just a way of life, and that's their team. Bart used to say that this is a very unique place, and he was always right. There's nowhere like it.

Lynn Dickey

Phil Epps. Dallas, 1984.

The regimes change with the Packers. We've gone through how many here over the years that Vernon's been covering the Packers? And yet he continues to do his best work every time that he goes out there. Nothing from the outside will ever affect what he does in trying to get the picture that he wants.

He says that at the end of every season he looks back over his work to see if he got that one great shot. Vernon is a guy of such strict high standards that I suspect that he never finds that one shot, and that's what directs him toward the next year to go after it, to keep looking.

JIM IRWIN

WTMJ Radio

During some periods, during down periods, I've almost lost interest, but finally what I'm interested in is the photography. It was photography itself that always kept me going. As long as I've been covering the Packers, I'm always hoping they will win, but more than that, I'm always looking for the one picture. If I can get one good picture a year, I'm happy.

VERNON BIEVER

Barty Smith. Detroit, 1976.

I remember the quote about Barty Smith in our highlight film from one year, "Barty Smith: more punishing than a Green Bay winter." And he really was. He was one of those players who played for the love of the game, who played despite what pain he might be in, who flung himself into the game. You know, people talk about how the players are bigger now, faster and stronger. I don't think they're tougher. And that may be one of those sour grapes theories, but I really look at the kind of code of honor that guys had. You play until the bone is sticking through the flesh or until you just can't get up, and anything short of that is inexcusable. Barty Smith was our team's warrior when I first got there.

JAMES LOFTON

I knew Barty Smith really well. Him and Eric Torkelson. Oh boy, was he tough. I really loved to have him on my field goal team. Boy could he block. He and MacArthur Lane.

CHESTER MARCOL

Lynn Dickey. Los Angeles, 1981.

People don't really give Dickey the credit he's due. You know, he was hurt all the time. Still no one threw a more pure pass than Dickey, and if you look at his record, his percentages are fantastic.

GARY KNAFELC

People don't know what Lynn Dickey went through coming back from that broken leg. I never believed that he was going to play football again because I seen him limping, walking with a cane. Yet I saw him work so hard in the training room to get ready. I was amazed that he was able to come back and continue to play as he did, and even with so many surgeries. He had a great arm and was a great all-around player.

CHESTER MARCOL

Me, James Lofton, and John Jefferson, also Eddie Lee Ivery and Gerry Ellis, there really wasn't any one person you could key on, and everybody complimented each other well. I was the go over the middle guy, James was the deep threat, John was the jitterbug-possession type, I mean, if you threw up the ball he was going to get it. Then Gerry and Eddie coming out of the backfield just added a whole different dimension. We basically had five wideouts. You see these teams go to this run and shoot, they put five receivers in. Well then the other team puts five d.b.s in to cover them. What we had, in essence was five receivers out there, but they were try-ing to cover myself and the running backs with linebackers, and it just couldn't be done. There were a few that could do it. Wilbur Marshall was one, and Lawrence Taylor could run with anybody, but for the most part you just couldn't cover myself or the running backs with linebackers. Or if they tried to double J.J. and James—which the Redskins tried to do—and go one-on-one with me with the strong safety, it was the same thing. Lynn and I would look at each other and almost bust out laughing.

PAUL COFFMAN

We talked about strategy a lot. I was the kind of player as quarterback that would really leave nothing unsaid during the week. I would say, "Listen, it's one thing to talk about this with the coaches, but you and I are the ones who are going to be on the field and we're going to have to do it." So during the week we always had very open discussions about a thing. It's amazing how many teams and players go on and don't talk about things and just expect that everybody knows it come Sunday. Sometimes that works, but why take a chance? I didn't want anybody to think; I wanted them to know exactly what we're all doing, and it worked.

LYNN DICKEY

Dickey was, as a pure passer, the best.

FUZZY THURSTON

Lynn Dickey. Detroit, 1984.

Pain is part of the game. I talk to people now and they say, "Well, you know, I would have played, but I hurt my knee," or, "I would have played, but the coach wasn't fair when I was in high school; he stuck me some-place that I'd never played before." You know, all of that is part of the game. I mean, it's a violent game, it's a game of adversity, it's a game of you're only as good as your next play. So basically, whether your last play was bad, whether your last year or last game you got injured, you've got to be able to overcome that and come back next week. It's just part of it. The injuries, missing balls, being able to shake it off.

PAUL COFFMAN

There was a certain magic about Lynn Dickey in that here was a guy who had been injured so badly he was never supposed to play again. Intestinal fortitude was one of those terms that was bandied about a lot in the sixties. Well, Lynn Dickey was the guy who embodied that in the seventies and eighties. He wasn't going to let "football injuries" stop him from being an NFL quarterback.

JAMES LOFTON

I guess I got beat up pretty good, and I had a lot of things that bugged me. My neck and lower back, taking injections for a broken transverse process in my back. I heard last year that that happened to somebody, bro-ken transverse process in the back, and they'll be out for two or three weeks, they put them on injured reserve. And I'm thinking back to 1984, when that happened to me, and I still remember, I mean, that hurt bad. To the point where you could barely catch your breath, it hurt to breathe. I went in the next day, and I remember Forrest Gregg said, "Well, I talked to the doctor, and he said that you can't injure yourself any more, it's just going to hurt."

And I said, "Well, they're right about that."

He said, "We need you to continue to play."

And I said, "Well, I'm going to be out there if I can."

The way I looked at it, it was just a part of it. There was never any doubt about just missing and sitting out. It wasn't an option.

I called it the twilight zone. When you're running during the summer before you go to training camp, you get to a point where you think you're going to die. A huge percentage of us grab the reins and pull back—"Oops, I don't think I'm going to go over into that new zone. I have never been over there." But a few of us say, "Screw it, I'm going to keep going and I'm going to see how far I can push myself, and I'm going to push myself to the point of total exhaustion, the point that I think that I am going to die, and I don't care. I'm out here to win and to do my very best, and you go beyond that."

It's true, mind over matter.

"Hey, I've got something hurting! Something's hanging off and dangling!"

Well, tape an aspirin to it and let's go.

LYNN DICKEY

James Lofton. Green Bay, 1981.

Once in a while a guy comes along, and I call 'em, well, they're just weird. Not as a person, but in their abilities. You just kind of look around at your other teammates and shake your head and say the guy is weird. I mean, normal people just aren't supposed to do these things that James could do on a football field. He was unique. It doesn't happen very often that someone comes along like that. He just had the physical talents and toughness. He was an amazing guy, he really was.

LYNN DICKEY

Pass catching for me wasn't just a hand-to-eye type of thing. It was more of a total body experience. You had to put yourself in the position, to understand the defense, to run the route, to get down the field. You didn't really have to focus on the ball, you just make the catch. It's a game of movement versus counter movement. And catching the ball was like taking someone else's man on the chess board. It's just the final element of it. You captured the ball, and catching the ball was just as simple as taking their man off of the chess board.

You would use everything. You would use all the film study that had gone on prior to the game. In the actual game there's a lot of communication that goes on between the quarterback and the wide receiver and the coach who is involved with the passing game, normally the offensive coordinator. You have conversations about what you want.

There's an old adage, "we'll take what the defense gives us." Well, for really dominant receivers, you take what you want. And that's the way we approached our passing game. We were going to go deep over the middle, deep to the outside, and we were going to do it regardless of whether or not the defense wanted to let us do it.

You know, you don't make every play, but you line up as if you're going to make every play. And then regardless of whether or not you've made ten in a row, you still approach the next one as the new one.

JAMES LOFTON

Lofton could run against anybody and he could catch the ball anywhere. Very strong upper body, a great receiver. That Washington game, he and Dickey were unbelievable. It was like a tennis match with the ball flying all over the place. They had some great games. And also the one in the snow against, I think it was Tampa Bay. It was snowing a tremendous blizzard, and Lofton had a fantastic day catching the ball for an astronomical amount of yards. Those two had great days.

GARY KNAFELC

Paul Coffman. Milwaukee, 1984.

As the tight end, they would beat the hell out of me all the way down the field. Just getting off the line of scrimmage was a major accomplishment. The linebacker beat the hell out of you, then the safety picked you up, he was right there.

GARY KNAFELC

Paul Coffman was an All-Pro, but I think the world of him because I had to go against him every day in practice. Here was a guy who worked, you know, gave everything he had.

MARK MURPHY

I wasn't drafted. Nobody wanted me. I was too small and too slow, and I played for a bad college team. We won one game my junior year and one game my senior year. And I was 6'3", I weighed, I think when they came and tried me out, maybe 212, maybe 215 pounds. And I ran about a 4.8 forty. So really, I wasn't like a talent, but apparently they were impressed with the way I worked out, and they needed people just to make the lines long in camp, you know, so the starters and the other people who were actually going to play during the season wouldn't get worn out during two-a-days. So that's kind of the reason I got invited to camp. The next year I led the team in receptions, led the NFL for tight end catches.

PAUL COFFMAN

I think it's a good analogy, Coffman to Fuzzy Thurston, because Coffman certainly was tenacious. He had glue on his hands. He wasn't fast, he didn't run great routes, he wasn't particularly in the open when the ball got delivered to him, but he didn't drop many. Whatever he had to do to catch it.

KEN BOWMAN

A scout came to Kansas State to look at Paul's roommate, and Paul just asked if he could tag along. When the scout looked at his roommate, Paul asked if he could run and catch some passes and run some pass patterns for them. He just kind of butted his way in there. And they took a look at him, and, well, this guy's got a lot of enthusiasm, and he's tough, and so they signed him and gave him a shot. If he hadn't butted his way in there he probably never would have gotten a shot. And that's how he conducted his career. He was very, very reliable. He and I had such a good quarterback-receiver relationship. I always seemed to know what he was thinking, he knew what I was thinking, we were always on the same page. I remember many times he would come back to the huddle and we would look at each other and laugh and say, "Boy, this is like cheating. It's so easy, and they can't get us out." He had a great, great feel for the passing game.

LYNN DICKEY

Green Bay, 1978.

Cold weather got to be commonplace, you know, when you play up in the Midwest and it gets into late November, early December. You get that frost coming through there, and you're alright maybe in the first half, but when you come back out of the locker room for the second half, all those chunks of grass, you understand, that had thawed were frozen. It was like ice picks sticking up in you. It did help, though, to be a hitter and not to be hit. It helped a heck of a lot.

WILLIE WOOD

It's a very intimidating factor when someone comes to Green Bay late in the season. When you live up here your blood thickens, but if you don't, you've got thin blood. Your fingertips go numb, you can't catch balls. It's great.

BRIAN NOBLE

It's good for the psyche of the people up there in Green Bay, you know. They understand it. It is an edge for a home team. We knew that when we played the Dallas Cowboys that Bob Hayes would never catch a pass in that, and he never did. He never made a catch against the Packers as a consequence.

PAUL HORNUNG

Coming from the South, it was hard to adjust to the weather at first. You don't get totally used to it, but being here three years, you know it's your home and it's where you've got to play. You know how to dress and how to handle it, how to practice in it so you can use it as an advantage. And we try to use it to our advantage the best we can. And we hope it will be really, really cold in January.

GEORGE TEAGUE

In those days we had to play outdoors in Minnesota. We had to play outdoors in Detroit. So, you know, we were lucky to play indoors once every three years, in the beginning. You could always figure on below zero in Minnesota and a couple games in Green Bay. I remember one time we went to play the last game in Atlanta; it was forty degrees and raining like crazy. I thought it was half summer, you know? It was a treat to play in.

CHESTER MARCOL

Denver, 1984.

You've just got to do it. It's going to be cold, and there's nothing you can do about it. But when it happens, you realize that the other teams hate it worse than you do. And luckily, I have big hands and I have a strong arm, so I can kind of fight through the wind and all that stuff, so I guess I'm just fortunate. Also, we play pretty well in those kind of conditions.

BRETT FAVRE

Forrest's favorite statement to us as players was, "Ah cain't control tha weatha!"

Once it was so cold we couldn't stand up, and another time it was snowing so hard we couldn't see. You were more concerned with staying warm out there than you were about practice. Don't fall down, because you had so much clothes on that you were like a turtle, you go out there and fall down, you need help to stand back up again.

BRIAN NOBLE

I saw a lot of guys fall in the snow, offensive players, sloppy fields and things like that. I think, once again, that it was that competitive drive. You just added another element to it, the weather, and did not to succumb to it.

JAMES LOFTON

The climate gave us an edge. No question. You can't get used to that kind of cold in one day. We had to practice in it all week, and sometimes it was so cold we could only practice an hour. Tears would come to your eyes, and they would freeze before they could drop off your face. It was unbelievable. And you're out there all bundled up in thermal underwear, Vaseline on our faces, we had on so many tee-shirts and sweatshirts, you couldn't even move. You catch somebody in Green Bay, like from Florida or California, you catch a team like that in that cold, you've got an edge. It's a mental thing. It's so cold, you don't even want to be out there, so you know the other chumps don't want to be.

Running in snow, you had to shorten your stride, you couldn't extend. But you know in Lambeau Field they have that heater under the field. It would make the field muddy, but you could still run in it a little bit. It wasn't frozen. Now, when we played that game in '72 up in Minneapolis, you know for the division championship, man, that was like running on concrete. You couldn't find a hole, you couldn't find a soft spot, you had to find cleat marks from previous games and stick your cleat in those to get some traction. It was the worst. And that wind would come hawking through there. When you hit it, oh my goodness. It was the pits, a baseball field. It was rough, man. It was rough.

JOHN BROCKINGTON

Brian Noble. Dallas, 1989.

Talk about a drastic change. In the Fall of '84 I had played UCLA in Phoenix, and it was 118 degrees on the field. And then the next year I played Tampa Bay here and it was twenty below.

In the locker room I'm watching these guys get dressed. You know, Ezra and John Anderson, all these guys are putting on Vaseline, nylons, all this stuff, and I'm going, "What are you guys doing?"

And they say, "Hey, man, be ready for it, because it's going to get cold out there."

So I followed suit and did my thing and we go out there.

These guys, Tampa, come out and they're running around, "Raahrr." And you look at these guys, and you know how all the linemen love to be all buffed up and they like to show their guns, their arms, so they wear jerseys with high sleeves. I believe Steve Courson was playing for them, who at the time was the strongest man in the world and all this stuff, well certainly strongest man in the National Football League anyway. So these guys come out, and I'm looking at them and I go, "Oh man, these guys are huge!"

Well, by five minutes into the first quarter their arms were blue. They were sore, they didn't want to be touched, and then it started snowing. Steve Young was their quarterback then, and they got mad at Steve if he called a timeout or if he passed the ball. They wanted him literally to run the clock out. I remember Sean Farrell getting mad at him.

"Just run the play, dammit! We want to get out of here!"

They were so cold that they didn't want to hit anything; they didn't want to fall on the ground. They were just cold and they wanted to leave.

And we were laughing, we were just dying. Alphonso Carreker tackled Steve Young, and he couldn't see out of his mask he had so much snow in it. It was just a gas.

To be honest, I just had fun playing football. You know, it really didn't make a difference if there was fifteen inches of snow on the ground or if it was ninety degrees down in Tampa. I just could not believe I was playing football in the National Football League. I was having fun.

BRIAN NOBLE

To play middle linebacker is very physical, and Brian Noble was a very physical player. A great run stopper.

RAY NITSCHKE

Brian Noble was probably one of the finest run-stuffing linebackers in the game. He's going to stuff the guard, he's going to take on the blocker. Noble was one of those guys who would take charge out there. He made the game fun too. A real emotional guy.

MARK MURPHY

We were a team that you had to play. We knocked the tar out of people.

BRIAN NOBLE

Tim Harris. Green Bay, 1989.

Timmy enjoyed the game of football. But it was tough to call signals in the huddle with Timmy there, because he was nonstop, sixty minutes, go. Mouth moving, body moving, arms moving, hands, I mean, we called him "The Alien." We had defenses designed specifically around Timmy, to give Timmy the flexibility to go wherever he wanted to go. Teams didn't know where he was going to hit you from. He was a tremendous football player. And very loud. We were playing in Cleveland Timmy's rookie year. Forrest was head coach, and I think at the time we were 0 and 7. All the sudden the coach decides, okay we're making changes. They were going to move me back inside and put Timmy on the outside and let it fly, you know, we were beyond the point of concern. Timmy goes out there with us, rookie guy, you know, kind of a lanky, tall, skinny kid out there. Just non-stop talking. Lining up over Ozzie Newsome, you know, Hall of Famer and all that stuff. Timmy's just jawing at Ozzie Newsome.

"You ain't nothin', you ain't da-da-da-da-da. . . ."

Ozzie looks up at me and says, "Hey Brian. Who is this guy anyway?"

Timmy wouldn't study a playbook, Timmy wouldn't do nothing. Timmy went out and had fun. He played football. And he did great against Cleveland. Two sacks. Had a great game.

BRIAN NOBLE

We revered Tim a lot. He had great strength, he could bull-rush when he had to, could speed rush. Timmy had a lot of moves. He was a guy you've got to feature, because, I mean, he creates havoc in there and makes big plays. Teams had to know where he was, and that was great. You always try to free up a guy like that too so they can't double team him, keep putting him on the weak pass blocker. Timmy talked a lot during games. His philosophy was he was going to try to take you out of your game, and if he knows it's bothering you, oh, you're going to hear it. Definitely give him his due. You can't deny his numbers.

MARK MURPHY

Chuck Cecil. Green Bay, 1991.

With Chuck Cecil, I guarantee you, you didn't want your head sticking out or he'd knock if off. I liked the way he played. When you're an end, if you're wandering around there and you know Chuck's around, sometimes you have a tendency to worry about him instead of catching the ball, and that's part of being a tough safety man.

MAX MCGEE

Chuck was very intense. Made some spectacular hits, and not all of them on the other team either. In a Dallas game he dislocated my sternum, cracked me one right in the ribs. Another time in L.A. I was throwing Eric Dickerson on the ground, and I twisted, and right when I twisted to throw Eric down Chuck just plowed me right in the hip. I got a sizeable hip-pointer out of it, and he said, "Aw, man, I'm sorry. . . ." That was just the way Chuck hit. We were so scared of him hurting himself, and then the fact that he'd hurt most of us, you know, kind of made us leary of Chuck. It was, "Okay, where's Chuck at? Chuck, where you coming from, buddy?" Wished we could put a cow bell on him so we could hear him coming. We liked to stand guys up so Chuck could come in and blast 'em, but it was almost like you had to put a target on them, the way that Chuck came in. You didn't want to make any movement to one side or the other at all because Chuck was like a train coming and he couldn't get off the track.

BRIAN NOBLE

Chuck could light you up, man. Here was a guy who was 180 pounds and just running through people. And I don' t just mean making a tackle, I mean running through them. Pound for pound he'd hit you harder than anyone in that league. Wouldn't back down from anybody. And it's fun if you've got two guys who can anchor the middle of the field and know that if somebody comes across the middle they're going to get pounded. That helps. Makes arms shorter. Chuck was intense, loved to play the game and had fun.

MARK MURPHY

Mark Murphy. Green Bay, 1991.

Mark Murphy was tougher than nails. A consistent, a week-in, week-out guy.

MAX McGEE

Murph was a 110-percent guy. He went out and gave you everything he had. He may not have been the fastest guy out there, but he used his head. He was a smart football player. I learned from guys like Mark Murphy and John Anderson. They studied so much that they knew every situation, so they could limit what could happen, and it made them better football players. Murphy was a very intense guy. Nights of games we didn't get a whole lot of sleep. We were up most of the night thinking. I think Lindy said it best when he said, "If I can have forty-seven Mark Murphys, I wouldn't have to worry about the Super Bowl at all." He was that kind of guy. Whether you're going out on a football field or you're in a bar fight, Mark Murphy's a guy that you want on your side.

BRIAN NOBLE

Guys like Mark Murphy and myself and Larry McCarren, we were pretty similar players. I was standing on the sidelines with Larry McCarren watching one of the alumni games, and he looks at me and he goes, "Wouldn't it have been great to play this game with talent?" You know because myself, and Murph and Larry, we were intensity guys. We had to be up for the game, we had to prepare during the week, we had to prepare with the playbooks, with the film. We didn't have the overwhelming speed or talent or strength to go out there and make mistakes and then catch back up. If we made mistakes, we got beat. We just went out there with intensity.

PAUL COFFMAN

I had the ideal job, a job that I loved to do, that I'd played for twenty-three years of my life. I wasn't getting paid for it in junior high or high school or college, but then all the sudden they're handing me a check? To play a game I love!

There were a lot of fun games. That's all that I know, you know, you go out and hit people, and I can honestly say that I enjoyed every game that I played in. It was fun.

And then you try to find something that is anywhere close to that when you get out of the game. It's hard for a lot of guys. It was hard for me. But coaching has helped, being able to keep a hand in it and hopefully make a difference in some kids' lives, and maybe share some things that you've learned over the years that people have shared with you. That's what I hope for. And you hope you can win some games along the way. I think that's what it's all about.

MARK MURPHY

Don Majkowski. Milwaukee, 1990.

I really liked Majkowski, you know. I liked him and thought he was a lot of fun. Scrambling and all, he used to get those key first downs. If he couldn't find somebody open, he'd get 'em himself. He would do the things it took.

MAX McGEE

Majkowski and Sharpe was kind of short lived, but still, they had some great games, didn't they? The game against the Bears that he threw that last-second touchdown to beat them was fantastic. That will go down as one of the all-time great Packer games.

GARY KNAFELC

Don Majkowski, Sterling Sharpe,
Brent Fullwood. Green Bay, 1989.

I think the '89 season got some excitement going for the Packers, set the stage. Number one, Majik did something. He was one of those scramblers. Especially that Bear game where he threw it with one foot half going to the line of scrimmage, but there was so much he did, so many things for that team. I think it did get some excitement going and people thinking about, well, maybe somewhere in this generation we're going to have another championship team.

MAX MCGEE

Nineteen eighty-nine was just scratching the surface. We had done something at that time that hadn't been done prior to that, going back to the sixties.

BRIAN NOBLE

Majik and Sharpe gave this team the excitement and desire to win that had not been here in twenty-five years. Both fierce competitors, they started to bring the Packers back to winning. They have their place in Packer history.

FUZZY THURSTON

Sterling Sharpe. Phoenix, 1990.

You know, when you play for Green Bay you have a 100-degree temperature swing during the course of the season. You'll play in the heat of Tampa, in 105 degrees, and you'll play in five above late in the year at Lambeau Field. So if you're a good receiver, you have to be a man for all seasons.

JAMES LOFTON

Sterling was a great player. He was definitely a big force in our offense. You know, I never threw to Sterling in practice? He was always too banged up. He was that good without practice.

BRETT FAVRE

Sharpe was truly a talent. His great talent was being able to run after catching the football. A better possession receiver than anyone. You could throw him a three-yard pass and he'd get that first down. He was really a hardnosed runner.

MAX McGEE

A brilliant football player.

MIKE HOLMGREN

You hear the broadcasters on television sometimes, and it's third and eight and they throw the ball out to a back, or let's say a tight end, running a pattern five yards downfield, and then they go ballistic saying, "Well, the guy didn't run his pattern deep enough!"

I just about, I'd like to turn the sound off, because that's ridiculous. It's the way the pattern is set up. And you can catch the ball and turn upfield and run for the first down. I mean, you get the ball under your arm, you're supposed to do something with it besides fall down.

Sterling Sharpe was the run-after-catch guy, but he had an awful lot of ability to get into the spots necessary to catch the ball. And he is a big, strong man. Big strong hands, and as far as taking the ball and turning up the field and running with it, I don't think I've seen anybody do it as physically. Very difficult to tackle. He turned into a running back after he caught the ball, a very strong running back, and very competitive in doing it. He could still go deep, he had deep speed, but I liked him because he was not one of these scrawny little guys running around out there. He's far from that. A lot of times people talk about receivers and they kind of laugh and say something about how they're, you know, not real football players, they're just receivers, they're just kind of like track guys, but he dispelled that notion very quickly. He was tough, the whole package, a pleasure to watch. I liked his competitiveness, and I have a lot of respect for him. He was a wonderful player.

BOYD DOWLER

Mike Holmgren. Green Bay, 1995.

Wolf and Holmgren are doing a tremendous job. They stabilized a lot of things. You know, if you have the ballplayers and you win, then everyone's got a good attitude, but they are the ones that went about building up the foundation. We're on the right track. I believe very much in these people.

TONY CANADEO

Mike Holmgren is blessed with huge common sense. It's amazing how many coaches there are in this league that are running these franchises that don't have it, but he's got it.

LYNN DICKEY

Mike Holmgren is upfront, and he's got a great sense of humor, but he's nobody to fool around with. He's very serious about what he does. If you're in his organization, you realize that. He's the best head coach in handling the media that we've ever had here, and I've been around all eleven of them at one point or another.

He knows how to be a head coach, and that's not given to everybody. There are a lot of guys who have been head coaches in this league who probably shouldn't have been, but he's a guy who really knows how, and that's perfectly evident in the way he handles his team. It's a hell of a challenge to try to coach a football team these days.

LEE REMMEL
Green Bay Packers Executive Director of Public Relations

I'd much rather be in a situation like this with the media. I was drafted by the New York Jets, so I've seen both ends of the spectrum.

CRAIG HENTRICH

Mike is one of the reasons why I came to Green Bay. I wanted to play here because I think Mike can lead this team.

REGGIE WHITE

Mike Holmgren. Green Bay, 1995.

I'm pretty conservative in my approach to what I think is good for the team and team unity. Make sure they understand what's expected of them. Stay consistent with your philosophy, and don't take any shortcuts.

MIKE HOLMGREN

I think Holmgren's great. He's the right man at the right place, right now. I think he's a great coach, and set up with Wolf as general manager and Bob Harlan as president, I think that other than Lombardi they're the best organization for getting something done that the Packers have had.

MAX MCGEE

I really like Mike. I've had a chance to visit with him several times during our fantasy camps. One of the things that Mike Holmgren has done that's, I think, indicative of his intelligence, is to include the former Packers, which not only includes the players, but includes the history and the tradition and the stories and all the things that that brings to an organization. If you look at any great business, they have a history and a tradition and a story line that follows them down through the years, and it makes them stronger. I think that's very bright of Mike to do that. Instead of an antagonistic relationship, now we're a part of the group again, and we're kind of a part of the family, and we've been included and it's very pleasant. The kids, when you chat with them, they're polite, they're respectful. It's just pleasant to visit with them. It's a nice relationship there.

JERRY KRAMER

Mike does a fantastic job of understanding players. He knows when to give players time to mend and to get well. He's very aware that players need time to recuperate, and he understands that. He makes sure his players are focused on what needs to be accomplished.

BRIAN NOBLE

I'm in the best place for a coach that I can be.

MIKE HOLMGREN

Reggie White. Green Bay, 1995.

When you start talking about Reggie, you're talking about the all-time all-time category.

WILLIE DAVIS

Reggie White is the most revered athlete I've ever been around.

DON BEEBE

Running onto Lambeau Field for the first time was exciting. I was just excited about playing and playing here. I was excited about being involved with the tradition of this team and the great players of the past. You've got to feel that you want to be a part of that.

REGGIE WHITE

Knowing that you're always going to have roster changes from season to season, you also know that you have a pretty good chance to keep your core group together—your team leaders. The people that will help you mold the new guys. The trick is targeting the right guys for your core.

MIKE HOLMGREN

Before I got here, I thought this guy is like God in pads, but meeting him, he's the most humble guy. He doesn't think he's better than anybody else. In this day and age of athletes, it's very rare to see.

DON BEEBE

Reggie White. Green Bay, 1995.

I've dedicated myself to this game. I've done my best to make the teams and the league look good. I go out and bust my behind to make sure that I come in prepared to help my team win, and I represent the league with the utmost of integrity and character.

I go out and work to try to accomplish that.

REGGIE WHITE

What a horse. What a great influence he's been on the organization.

JERRY KRAMER

Reggie White is probably the best defensive lineman that's ever played.

BRIAN NOBLE

Reggie White has an amazing effect on the younger players. Guys on the fence who can go either way are going to go the good way because of Reggie.

DON BEEBE

Reggie White. Green Bay, 1995.

I'm insulted when I hear people say, "Defenses have just gotten too good. That's why we have to change the rules."

That's an insult because the guy on the other side of the ball is required to work just as hard as I do. When you take something away from me, saying that he doesn't have to work as hard, it's an insult to me, but it's an insult to him too. For you to take it away from me, you're saying I'm in better shape than the guy across from me, and the only way he can stop me is to do illegal things.

You cannot convince me, you'll never be able to convince me, that fans only respond to high scores. The intelligent fan understands defense.

REGGIE WHITE

The game of football is not as simple as it might seem. There are reasons for everything. Reasons for everything that happens in football. It's complicated, the reasons for blocks and defenses, and everything else, but by understanding it better, by knowing the intricate parts, fans enjoy it more.

JIM TAYLOR

They make all of these rule changes. When you can stick both hands out on an opposing lineman you know it's so easy to close that hand when the guy is getting away, and they don't call that stuff. And they're doing all of that to protect quarterbacks because they think that's their marquee player. But I say get yourself four or five quarterbacks. And that's what the coaches are for. Football strategy is a cat and mouse situation. If they've got a new defense, you figure out a way to beat it.

Once you start legislating safety for quarterbacks and all that stuff, it takes away from the game.

MAX McGEE

In my opinion, allowing them to extend their arms has made offensive linemen today a little lesser in skills than they were when I was playing. You look at the Forrest Greggs and Bob Skoronskis of the world, and these guys actually blocked people with their forearms and shoulders, their hands inside their body width, and really got the job done. They got it done with good footwork and balance. They were really technically so much superior to what you see today. The strategy seems to be to get big people and just try to get them to stay in the way, as much as anything, by holding.

What is crazy in the NFL is that every team that starts to win sets a trend. Whether it's big backs or big receivers or big linemen, pretty soon everybody else gravitates toward that. I think that size for size's sake is almost out of control in the NFL. You've got guys in much less shape because they're so concerned about being big and huge that I think the skill level has dissipated.

WILLIE DAVIS

Reggie White. Green Bay, 1993.

Reggie White is just an all-around player. He can do everything. Reggie's the type of guy that elevates everyone around him up another notch.

MIKE McCoy

Of course Reggie is all-world. There's no doubt about it. He does some things that I've never seen other people do.

MAX McGEE

The thing you've got to learn to do as you play this game is to adapt to what you've got. And you've got to keep a focus. This is a business, and you know it's going to change, so you have to always prepare yourself for change.

REGGIE WHITE

When Reggie White came in here, that signaled to the rest of the National Fooball League that the Packers are for real and, more importantly, that Green Bay is for real.

RON WOLF

In this day and age, I can assure you that Reggie White is the real thing. What he says, he means.

MIKE HOLMGREN

Brett Favre. Green Bay, 1995.

You sure as hell have got to love Brett. You just have to love everything about him. His athletic ability, the way he competes, his style, love his attitude. I really am excited about him. I'm excited about all of them, I can't wait for the season to start.

JERRY KRAMER

I think Favre is a physical talent. Everybody that's ever been a receiver for the Packers says that the guy can throw the ball through a concrete wall, and it looks like he can. And then you see these quarterback matchups in the off-season and he's tossing the ball seventy, seventy-five yards in the air. He's just a physical talent.

KEN BOWMAN

The day you start thinking you're the best and you'll be here forever is the day you'll lose your job. It keeps me on the top of my game, and that's where I want to stay for a long time.

BRETT FAVRE

Brett is fiery, competitive, excitable. He rejoices when something good happens. He gets mad when something bad happens. But he has also shown the ability now to maintain his composure and continue to play at a high level. He might do it in a little more unorthodox fashion at times, he'll break the pocket more, make the great plays from awkward positions, but he has the physical tools to do that.

MIKE HOLMGREN

Brett Favre. Green Bay, 1995.

In Green Bay it seems like everybody from the top to the bottom is on the same page. From Bob Harlan down to the trainers and equipment guys, everybody's on the same page, and that's important in the goals that we want to achieve and in what we'll be able to achieve. There's a winning attitude here. People want to win. People have proven that they want to win, and that's important.

REGGIE WHITE

Favre is what football is all about. Love for the game, very competitive, love for his teammates, gutsy, full of courage, a passion for making the Packers the best team in football and blessed with a great arm and a passion to win at all costs. Favre is my man.

FUZZY THURSTON

I hear about the Packers now being America's team, and I think that's real accurate. Dallas has been a great football team, obviously, just by their Super Bowls. But I wish I had a nickle for every time last year someone said, "I wish it was y'all instead of Dallas," and not just in Green Bay. I've been to New York, I've been to Los Angeles, everywhere, and people have said, you know, "We want y'all to win." I went to the Super Bowl in '95, didn't go to the game, but everyone there was like, "We wish you were here instead of Dallas." Once again, I think they're a great team, and maybe sometimes that pisses people off. When you're so good people kind of get a little jealous and envious.

BRETT FAVRE

Brett Favre. Green Bay, 1995.

Vince and Holmgren were both offense coaches, so I think they probably have a stronger relationship with their quarterbacks than some other coaches might. I know Holmgren does because he has brought Brett along pretty much under his personal tutelage. I'd think Holmgren and Favre have had a good relationship. Lombardi had the iron fist; he was tough on Bart. I would imagine it's probably a little jollier with Holmgren than it was with Vince, who had a way of, you know, when he talked to you, well, it was not like a father and son banquet, let me put it that way.

MAX MCGEE

We've had some ups and downs, but to get to where we are now we had to go through that. It wasn't easy for me, and I know it wasn't easy for Mike, but we fought through it. He was patient enough to keep me in there. And now he trusts me, I trust him. He's going to make the right decisions, and he obviously trusts me to make the right decisions. And he kind of puts a little bit of a burden on my shoulders by saying, "Hey, if you want to audible, do it. But just don't make the wrong audible, and just be smart with it, but I'm going let you do that." And all of a sudden there's a lot of confidence both ways. And our relationship now is a hell of a lot better than it was a couple years ago.

BRETT FAVRE

Back in my first or second year, I thought I knew it all. But what I found out was that I didn't know anything. There were some tough times. But the one thing was he was very patient with me and he was fair. And now I respect him for that, and I realize that he was right.

BRETT FAVRE

Brett Favre. Green Bay, 1995.

They've got the best quarterback in the league right now, and if he keeps having years like that, one of these years he's going to jump up and beat everybody.

PAUL HORNUNG

Steve Young is so quick and fast, he has those great running abilities. But Favre's got a better arm. He's got a rifle. Bradshaw is a better comparison, really.

MAX MCGEE

This team has a lot of character, has great leadership, has a quarterback that is playing just as good as anyone in this league, has guys that have taken the right steps at the right time, and it's a team that doesn't have an ego. No one's jealous of each other, we're just having fun. We have guys who come into the locker room early just to come in and be with the guys. You know, we enjoy each other. And when that's happening you're capable of beating anybody, and you begin to build a legacy. If we continue to move in the direction that we're moving now and the team continues to build, then this will be the team to beat in the middle and late nineties.

REGGIE WHITE

How many times have we seen a guy who's on top of the world and a year or two later you never even hear from him anymore? So I always motivate myself by saying, "A couple of bad games, and you're easily forgotten." And that's true.

BRETT FAVRE

Robert Brooks. New Orleans, 1995.

I've enjoyed throwing to Robert. He has speed, he can go deeper. He's not as strong as some, but he's as durable as anybody.

BRETT FAVRE

It's a benefit of having all of us around here for five years. Brett knows what we're all going to do in certain situations. It makes it easy for us.

MARK CHMURA

Brooks is a great breakaway. He's always apt to bust one. Obviously a top man there now.

MAX MCGEE

Boy, he can run. Brooks can move, he's quick. He's a quality player.

BOYD DOWLER

Robert Brooks has become a great receiver. With his ability and desire, the future is very bright for this young man.

FUZZY THURSTON

Brooks has got great speed, but he runs great routes. Everyone says how fast he is, and that's nice, but he runs great routes. The great receivers don't ever do it just by speed. The great receivers, you look at all of them, ran great routes. Look at Fred Biletnikoff or Raymond Berry, they couldn't run a lick. Probably slowest guys on their ball clubs, but they ran great, great routes. You take that and add speed, and you've got something unique. Lofton had that, and this kid does.

GARY KNAFELC

You could put together a pretty good crew of guys out of the Packer receivers over the years. I don't know whether I'd rank third or fourth or fifth. Might be hard to get on the field. I might have to come in and play tight end on passing situations. That wouldn't be bad either. That wouldn't be a bad group. Play three wides, I'd be the inside guy. I'd be the slot receiver.

BOYD DOWLER

Mark Chmura. Green Bay, 1996.

Chmura's a good, solid player. He's a big guy and a good receiver, and they seem to communicate. Favre gets the ball to him real well. Good player.

BOYD DOWLER

Looks like he's a great tight end. He and Favre are roommates, I guess, so you know they kind of connect. That's kind of the way it was in '79, David Whitehurst and I were roommates, and any time he got in trouble he would look for me. That was kind of the connection there.

PAUL COFFMAN

I think he was a surprise to all of us. I had kind of said on the radio along the way that once they lost Jackie Harris they had to come up with a tight end. It's so important in their offense, especially against those zone defenses, somebody that can get in that seam. They put all their marbles on Chmura which is good, he's a good football player.

MAX MCGEE

I've been throwing to these guys, Robert and Chmura for four years, basically, but people go, "Where'd they come from?" Well, I've known them ever since I've been here. They're hard workers and they just bring something to the table that we haven't had here before, having the full number of receivers. Having the tight end, having the second receiver, having running backs who catch, it's been a lot of fun, and it enables this offense to work the way it's supposed to.

BRETT FAVRE

I've always liked Chmura. Three years ago I said he was the best tight end they've had here in a long time, and this is a team with a history of great tight ends. He's a guy who just loves to play the game. No one has more tenacity to go after the ball as hard as he does. He's a throwback. He could have played on our ball club with no problem at all. He's kind of like a Ron Kramer. Both he and Brett are throwbacks. They'd go out and play if nobody came to the game. And they'd play hard.

GARY KNAFELC

Chmura is a real outstanding man with many years of All-Pro status ahead of him. Great work habits and excellent attitude, which will make him a great football player for many years.

FUZZY THURSTON

Edgar Bennett. Green Bay, 1994.

I think Edgar is a good back in the fact that he takes on challenges. The media, the fans, the weather. You have to give him credit for that.

WILLIAM HENDERSON

When Edgar's running the ball, he hears me yelling for him. If I get an interception, he's the first guy to congratulate me.

LEROY BUTLER

We aren't a bunch of individuals who are selfish. We are a bunch of guys who want to go out there and win games. If you've got a lot of players who are playing well as individuals, you might as well be playing tennis or golf.

SANTANA DOTSON

We have had an unselfish group for the last two years, and I'm sure it has helped us win games. The idea that they don't care who gets the credit and they are happy for the other guy scoring the touchdown, I think, is a very healthy thing for any team to have.

MIKE HOLMGREN

I think a lot of people want to play in Green Bay now. The fact that we've been successful of late, and the way that the fans and the players are coming together makes the players want to come in and play.

ROBERT BROOKS

We had tremendous team attitude last year and that has to be maintained, starting right now until the end of the season.

MIKE HOLMGREN

They're close. They're getting closer every year. But how do you beat Dallas in Dallas? It looks as if every year to get to the Super Bowl you've got to go to Dallas, and it's pretty tough to win. That's their immediate problem.

PAUL HORNUNG

There's only one goal for this team, and that's the big one.

CRAIG HENTRICH

This was my most fun year coaching. So much is written about the spoiled professional athlete in all levels of sports and, you know, we're not perfect, but they really rooted for one another and helped each other out. And joking around in the locker room, it was a pleasant place to go into. It was one of those years you won't forget. But now the challenge for me is, let's do it again.

MIKE HOLMGREN

Dallas, 1994.

San Francisco, 1996.

They've had success, and sometimes success changes people. But the leaders, the Edgar Bennetts, the guys who came my first year, after the first, Brooks, Chmura, Bennett, all these guys, upbeat guys, they've still got a smile on their faces. It's not torture.

MIKE HOLMGREN

They're going to be one of the favorites to get there this year. They keep knocking on the door. The road through Dallas has been killing them, but you know they're going to get by that road one of these days.

See, to me, I've never put much significance on a so-called "tough schedule." You know, you gotta beat 'em all anyway, so what the hell's the difference. I'd just as soon play good teams. We normally played better against good teams anyway. Sure you've got to play Frisco and Dallas, but it makes you a better team.

MAX McGEE

They can say whatever they want, the Green Bay Packers are America's team, I don't care what they say about anybody else. And it will always be this way. The Packers will only get stronger.

GARY KNAFELC

Edgar Bennett. Green Bay, 1994.

People see the finished product, but they don't see the pain that football players go through. I mean, football is a tough game. I'm telling you, Manny Sistrunk weighed 260, but now the Manny Sistrunks of the league weigh 325, 340. This is a hard, hard game, and it is played by rough, tough people. And it is not easy. When you get a guy who weighs 300-something pounds and he wants to go left, you cannot stop him. The only thing you can do is help him get there faster, and a running back has to be able to run off the blocks. It is hard, and whether these guys are getting hit on turf or on grass, it doesn't make any difference, it takes a toll on your body.

JOHN BROCKINGTON

Edgar Bennet is a tough guy. He's looking for bigger and better things this year than he had last year.

MIKE HOLMGREN

Antonio Freeman. Green Bay, 1995.

And they've got some young kids coming along that are going to be all right.

MAX MCGEE

Teams really couldn't key on one player. I think that's what made us so successful last year. If they we're going to try and take Robert out, then Edgar or Antonio or I was there. Antonio Freeman came and filled in great. It's what this offense has to have. It's how you win championships.

MARK CHMURA

Getting the ball in more hands is what really helped our offense. It's what really helped us, I guess you could say, blossom. And the development of Brett as a quarterback, because Brett is the reason why the ball is spreading around.

EDGAR BENNETT

This could be the best group of receivers that a Packer quarterback has ever had. They've never had as good a young group as now, including the backs. Check the stats at the end of a game. Six guys have caught the ball, and it isn't like a two-yard completion here and a three-yard completion there, they're all catching for pretty good yardage.

GARY KNAFELC

By involving more players, they have a stronger feeling that they're contributing, and their level of play comes up.

MIKE HOLMGREN

Chris Jacke. Green Bay, 1994.

I presume I was the Packers first soccer-style kicker. There was no doubt that by far soccer style was more accurate, because you can control the ball better. The amazing thing was there were a lot of guys capable of doing what I was doing when I was in college. A lot of small schools, other NAIA schools, had soccer kickers, and yet University of Michigan against Ohio State lost two games on the last field goal because they didn't have a kicker.

CHESTER MARCOL

You're focused before you even step on the field. You go out there with the frame of mind that you're going to make the kick. You can never let it enter your mind that you're not going to. That's the frame of mind that you're in.

CHRIS JACKE

I have nothing but very positive things to say about Chris Jacke. His results speak for themselves. If you can do as well as he does kicking in Green Bay, that's a pretty amazing feat. Because I remember that even Jan Stenerud, after he came into Green Bay, he and I talked and he said, "Man, it's just hard to believe that you've played in this kind of climate, year after year."

CHESTER MARCOL

LeRoy Butler. Green Bay, 1991.

Defense wins in football. Defense wins, period. Offense might win some games, but defense wins championships. When I played early on in high school and in college, they always put their best players on offense, and the leftover players on defense. They changed that when they figured out that defense wins championships, so they put their best players on defense. And all the sudden you had guys like Jack Tatum playing defense, where years before he would have been an offensive player. Now they're always going to put good ballplayers on defense. Look at some of these guys on defense now. Some of these guys are as fast as running backs.

JOHN BROCKINGTON

I learned as a kid, "Eye on the ball, won't miss at all." I remember Dave Robinson one time, he says, "When I get a ball, I treat it like it's a dollar bill or it's my wallet." You go after that wallet, you go after that dollar bill. It's true in all sports, tennis, baseball, basketball. You keep your eye on the ball. I mean there's different techniques of catching it high or low and all that, but if you keep your eye on the ball, you can catch it anyway.

MARV FLEMING

Sean Jones. Milwaukee, 1994.

For some reason I just seemed to watch Sean Jones more last season, and I thought he came on real good. I thought that against some teams he was grossly underestimated. I was impressed with him.

MAX McGEE

I think that maybe the strongest part of Green Bay's team up front now are the two ends. Sean Jones and Reggie White get it done. They are playing at such a high level in today's game, but still you would have liked to have seen that pair of bookends playing in an earlier era of the game.

WILLIE DAVIS

I don't even know how the scouts found me, playing against James Madison, U Mass, and URI, before, if we were lucky, a whopping 2,300.

SEAN JONES

Craig Newsome. Green Bay, 1995.

It's different. We've got some great guys up here with great attitudes, and I think that's drawing more great players to the team.

EDGAR BENNETT

They've got a pretty good outfit in the secondary. They're pretty tough.

MAX McGEE

I think that right now, as a group, they're probably the finest young group of defensive backs in the National Football League. I think that in time, once they sort of develop and mature, they're going to be something to be reckoned with. I just hope that defenses can keep putting pressure on the offenses without any more of these rules adaptions. If that happens, they're going to be as good as they want to be.

WILLIE WOOD

Craig Hentrich. Green Bay, 1995.

We practice corner kicks two or three times a week. Just like anything else you get used to it, and you get accustomed to which way you have to step. Of course you've got to deal with the wind and things like that outside, but it's all practice. There are always a lot of situations that can go wrong, a block isn't made the right way or something where I have to step differently. So many things can go wrong. But all in all, it's just practice, repetitions. Once you get it down it's going to be there.

CRAIG HENTRICH

Hentrich has got a unbelievable leg.

CHESTER MARCOL

I'd just like to improve off last year. That's my goal every year, to get better every year and eventually be up there on the top. That's my long-range goal. Right now I just hope to get better.

CRAIG HENTRICH

John Jurkovic. Green Bay, 1993.

Obviously the change has been in the financial end of it and the exposure, the media, the attention. And the dominant head coach, like Lombardi, or like a lot of the other coaches, is a thing of the past. Different era, different time, different kids. But I don't think the game, inside the lines, has changed that dramatically. My feeling is that the things on the field, the actual contact, the qualities it takes to play the game, the type of kid that plays the game, the necessary ingredients to be a part of the whole thing are pretty much the same. Sideline to sideline, end zone to end zone, there's not a lot of changes. Kids are a little bigger, maybe a little faster, but we're still playing the same game, and they're still doing the same basic things.

JERRY KRAMER

I hated to see them lose Jurkovic. He was a good guy, a good team man, a favorite of mine.

MAX McGEE

George Teague. Green Bay, 1995.

It's a great stadium to play in. There's a lot of tradition, and the fan support is unbelievable. It's like no other place.

ROBERT BROOKS

I've been the PA announcer at Lambeau Field for thirty-two years now. In fact, Coach Lombardi gave me that job on the way home from the airplane when I retired.

Lambeau Field is still the best place to see a football game. There isn't a bad seat in the place.

GARY KNAFELC

You've got to agree with what's going on. Mike and Ron Wolf have built a pretty powerful machine. When Ron came in, he said his main focus, the number one thing that he wanted to do, was change the attitude of this football organization, and not just of the football players but of the entire organization. And think of the attitude that's here now. This is the place to be. You can even ask Mike Holmgren about back when he was coaching in San Francisco and a player wasn't doing something right or was having problems or something, it was, "Hey, we'll ship you off to Green Bay if you don't get your crap together." Well, now they don't have that problem. Now there is no threat to being "shipped to Green Bay." Because it would be, "Fine! Send me to Green Bay! I'd love to play in Green Bay!" They've done what they've needed to do to change the attitude of that football team. Ron did that, and Mike nurtured it. And the one thing you can't argue with is success.

BRIAN NOBLE

This is the place where I want to be. It's exciting. It's exciting to run out on the field before the game. We've got some wonderful fans here, a wonderful organization. If it's up to me, I'll play here for many more years to come.

GEORGE TEAGUE

This is now the garden spot of the league.

MIKE HOLMGREN

Scott Hunter. Green Bay, 1971.

The greatest thing about football then was that all of us played together for so long. That's a great thing for a quarterback to have, when you play with these guys probably about six, seven years, the same group. That's gone. You'll never have that again. The fans will never know the players in the same way, and the players will never know the fans. It used to be that back when you went out to dinner, people would walk up, and you knew them. You knew everybody in town. Of course Green Bay was smaller at that time, but still you get to know all these people. Walking down the street, driving your car, they'd wave to you. It was like the old college town.

GARY KNAFELC

That's what was nice for me about playing twelve years in Green Bay, to play with and be around a lot of the same people. And it's a family-oriented community and sports-minded. To see the fans and things develop and grow. That's what was fun.

MARK MURPHY

You can't say Packer fans are fair-weather fans because we don't ever have fair weather here. Come December it's pretty nasty. We went down to play Atlanta the last game of one year, and I think they were like, I don't know, 4-11. They had 13,000 people in the stands. We go 4-11, and our last game here on December 28 will still be sold out. Regardless of who we're playing! Dallas, when they're winning, that's great, they're America's team, blah, blah, blah. But if they're losing, nobody's there. They don't have 20,000 people in the stands, and they'll be giving seats away. Here, it doesn't make a difference, there are people coming from all over the country to sit in Lambeau Field, which is the place to watch football, to watch the Green Bay Packers.

BRIAN NOBLE

Green Bay, 1993.

The fans in San Francisco are awesome, New York, everyone has great fans. But here you get the feeling it's everybody. At times that's a burden that weighs heavily on me, but it's also something that's very great. Everybody is a part of this here.

MIKE HOLMGREN

I love him to death. Without Coach Holmgren, there would be nothing. He's just a great guy.

LEROY BUTLER

If you ever wanted to win a game for a coach, you'd want to win this one for him.

GILBERT BROWN

It's been a fun ride.

BRETT FAVRE

Green Bay, 1995.

Green Bay is like a college town in the way the fans are so nuts about the Packers. It's just a great place to play.

CRAIG HENTRICH

People relate to the underdog. Because of the size of Green Bay, and the fan ownership, they always include themselves as if it is their team.

FUZZY THURSTON

The thing about Green Bay is that they're totally dedicated to their football team. It didn't make any difference what our record was, and believe me, our record my rookie year, we were 4-8-2, but the last home game the stadium was packed. They love the team.

JOHN BROCKINGTON

Green Bay is like a college atmosphere. It's a great place to play, so much excitement. Football is it in this state. The fans back you, no matter what. Places like New England or New York, do one little thing wrong and they're jumping down your neck.

MARK CHMURA

The Packers will always have this love for their fans.

FUZZY THURSTON

There are educated fans all across the country, but in terms of being there no matter what the temperature or the climate, Packers fans are unparalleled. And by climate, I don't just mean the weather, but climate in terms of how your team is doing. That really differentiates them from other fans around the league. This Super Bowl run is new for the Packers, but the fan support isn't, and that definitely should be recognized.

SEAN JONES

Green Bay, 1966.

This probably isn't the place for everybody. I've talked to every potential free agent that we've had. I've said exactly the same thing to each one, from Reggie White to some that we didn't get. There's a certain uniqueness to this community that you don't find around the league. Its size being one thing, attitude being another. What the team means to the people being a third. Not just the demographic of males between the ages of nineteen and forty, those that typically watch football on television, but what the team means to every person. I tell them this is the way it is, and if you need more than that, if you need a New York City or Los Angeles, then this isn't the place.

MIKE HOLMGREN

I'm a firm believer that there are more Packer fans spread out across the country than any other team. Yeah, there's a lot of Cowboy fans down in the South, Southwest, but as far as the entire country, there's more Packer fans than anyone else.

BRIAN NOBLE

The whole state is with us. Until you live there and experience it, it's hard to describe. Every time we go on the road, there is a good group of people in green jerseys with those crazy Cheesehead hats on. It's nice to see, and it really helps the team.

MIKE HOLMGREN

I got started in the business at an early age, learning from my dad. He started taking me along to games when I was fourteen or so. He taught me positioning. It started out just following him around the first few years, learning where to be, where to go. I also saw that one of his best assets is his ability to get along with people. On the sidelines it's pretty impersonal. Photographers generally don't talk to anybody, but dad does and I think it helps the photography. He has a rapport with people that puts them at ease so there's no intrusion, and it allows him to work freely.

We'd come back from the game on Sunday night and he'd process the film, and just going through those pictures after a game I learned a lot. It's amazing, that tiny little darkroom has produced so many pictures. It's unbelievable. I learned composition just being able to see the pictures that he produced.

He was disciplined by the equipment he used before the .35 mm cameras into anticipating the precise moment to take the shot. It's called the "decisive moment," and it's a key thing to learn when you're starting out. For the Starr sneak picture at the Ice Bowl, I was using a single frame, almost amateur camera. I learned from him how you pick your shot.

That he's still working as hard as he does amazes everybody. Here's a guy who's seventy-four years old, and he insists on kneeling on the sidelines to get a slightly different, lower angle. And I say, "Dad, you can probably stand. They'll let you stand."

"Oh, no," he says, "I have to get this. It's a better angle."

JOHN BIEVER
Sports Illustrated

Miami, 1971.

Keith Jackson. Green Bay, 1996.

I looked at it as a bad thing being traded to Green Bay, but then once I got here, God worked it out for good. It's actually been a tremendous experience. I judged it for what you see on TV, the cold weather and no night life. And it is cold weather, and there's no night life. But then I started watching the team on the field, and I said I'm going to go in and play.

Reggie was a good friend and it's something to hear a good friend say, "Keith, forget about the cold, forget about everything you've heard." That's different than coming from a coach or administration that wants you in that place. When I got here, I wasn't disappointed. He was exactly right. I took his word for it.

Keith Jackson

Nobody has more weapons than we do. With this team, who are you going to stop? There are so many guys with big-play potential.

Dorsey Levens

What we have on offense are playmakers. Look at the names. We are very complementary. We have several guys who can make plays, and that makes it tough. Who do you double?

Antonio Freeman

We got guys off of football's skid row. We got guys who people said were too old, or too soft, or they were troublemakers, or washed up. And now look what happened. It just goes to show you that you never know what can revive a player.

Keith Jackson

That's how we played all year. Nothing different.

Antonio Freeman

You have a deep appreciation for this after all the years I've played and come up empty-handed. I was joking with the young guys, telling them, "I can't stand you guys. I had to wait nine years to get a ring, and you get it in only two years."

Keith Jackson

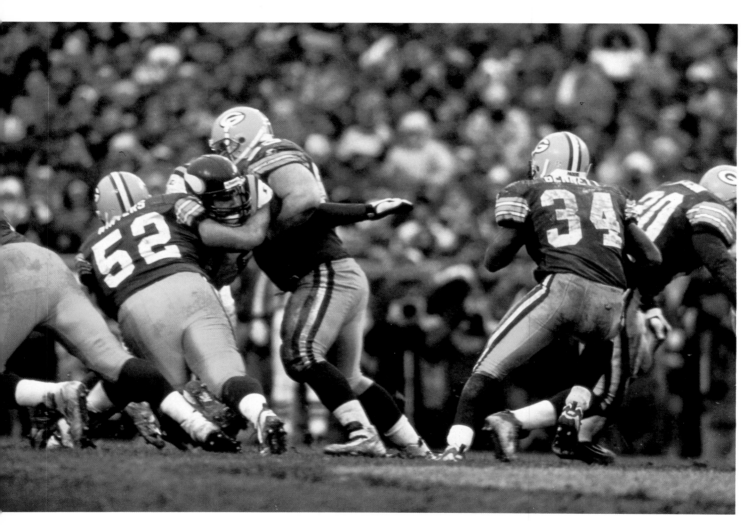

Edgar Bennett. Green Bay, 1996.

I think we showed the world what this offense is capable of.

ANDRE RISON

We still had a lot of unfinished business concerning Minnesota. There was a little too much jawing that came out of Minneapolis after that game. We felt we played well against that team. They acted like they steam-rolled us and blew us out. They have selective amnesia in terms of that game. If they're good enough to beat us, that will be fine. We'll show up and see what happens.

SEAN JONES

Minnesota is one of the teams that we really don't like that much.

LEROY BUTLER

Edgar likes the bad fields. There's no question. He was happy the other day when the snow started. He thinks he can stand up and just balance better than the people he's playing against.

SHERMAN LEWIS

Our biggest motivation all year was people said our weakest point was our running game. We've been hearing that all year. We haven't been respected all year, and we're not asking anybody to give it to us. We have to go out and take it.

DORSEY LEVENS

I think Edgar is a good back in the fact that he takes on any challenge. The media, the fans, the weather. You have to give him credit for that.

WILLIAM HENDERSON

When Edgar's running the ball, he hears me yelling for him. If I get an interception, he's the first guy to congratulate me.

LEROY BUTLER

Edgar Bennett. Green Bay, 1996.

Like my older brother. My big brother.

EDGAR BENNETT

These guys are the best. We all lean on each other.

DORSEY LEVENS

Dorsey is a great athlete and probably one of the best backs in the league as far as versatility is concerned.

EDGAR BENNETT

I had a good teacher. Edgar has taken me under his wing. We both want to do well. And in the process of a game, if one of us sees the other one running hard, it motivates the other one to run that much harder. I think we complement each other.

DORSEY LEVENS

We aren't a bunch of individuals who are selfish. We are a bunch of guys who want to go out there and win games. If you've got a lot of players who are playing well as individuals, you might as well be playing tennis or golf.

SANTANA DOTSON

We treat this as a family. We win as a family, we die as a family.

EDGAR BENNETT

We have had an unselfish group for the last two years, and I'm sure it has helped us win games. The idea that they don't care who gets the credit and they are happy for the other guy scoring the touchdown, I think, is a very healthy thing for any team to have.

MIKE HOLMGREN

Gilbert Brown. New Orleans, 1997.

I really try not to worry about preseason prognostications or anything like that. We just set our goals high and then tried to play one game at a time. You need a little luck and you have to avoid too many injuries, but we always knew we had a good team.

MIKE HOLMGREN

We have been challenged all year, and we have responded to every challenge.

SEAN JONES

I'm really excited for our team. What we've been through, what we accomplished.

BRETT FAVRE

We have pointed to this for so long and now it's here. I can't even describe it. This is the greatest feeling I've ever had. We finally got here. It was a long road. It was a little bumpy along the way, but we got here. That's all that matters now.

LEROY BUTLER

We got here through hard work and really dedicating ourselves to winning it all

MARK CHMURA

We win with class and we lose with class. We have fun, and people like to watch us play.

BRETT FAVRE

People have been counting us out all season, and that's fine. But we're the world champions now, and no one's going to take that away from us.

ANTONIO FREEMAN

I thank God I was able to step up when I did. Eugene Robinson kept coming up to me and saying, "Isaiah 40:31 says we must mount up with wings of an eagle, run and not get weary, walk and not get tired."

REGGIE WHITE

Mike Holmgren.   New Orleans, 1997.

Down there in the trenches, that's where the men play. That's the man's game. You've got everyone coming at you. I like playing nose tackle. It's my home.

GILBERT BROWN

We're not flashy, and we don't have national commercials. You don't see us on the front page of newspapers doing this, that, and the other thing. We're not sexy enough for everybody, but that's okay. Because you know what? When you wear that ring on your finger, there's a whole lot of people who think you're plenty sexy.

SEAN JONES

When Gilbert became available, we felt we had to look at him. I think we hit on one.

MIKE HOLMGREN

You can't move Gilbert Brown. I know. I play against him every day. Not only is he as big as a piano, he's as hard to move as one. And as much fun, too.

ADAM TIMMERMAN

My mom feeds all of us well. That's why I am the way I am today. People are amazed at how big I am. I tell them, that may be, but you don't know what you're missing. My mom cooks just about everything. Peppery steaks, fried chicken, what she cooks is so good that I just have to taste it.

GILBERT BROWN

He loves his mother. I'm glad he loves his mom. But she's too good a cook. I try not to let him go home.

MIKE HOLMGREN

Andre Rison. Green Bay, 1997.

I look at the faces of my players and my coaches and ownership in the locker room. I'm humbled by that, I'm overwhelmed by it. I think it's a great sense of accomplishment for the football team. I'm so happy for those guys. They worked very, very hard for this.

MIKE HOLMGREN

I don't care what anybody says, I think Mike Holmgren is the best coach in football right now. That was the greatest game plan I've ever come across. That man is a genius.

DON BEEBE

We've got the master coach. Mike Holmgren is a very smart man and a wonderful motivator. He is perfect for this team and he makes adjustments that give you a chance to win. We follow the leader here.

LEROY BUTLER

All week long I kept reading and hearing that Bill Parcells was some kind of demigod. Well, I'm very happy Mike Holmgren is coaching this team.

SEAN JONES

In Lambeau Field he is 30-4. In Lambeau Field, the man they named the trophy after was 28-6. Think about that. That's an incredible statistic. I'm not suggesting they rename the trophy, but it's time for him to get his due.

RON WOLF

I wish that we could bottle up what we do in the locker room, what we do all the time in Green Bay in showing high school and junior high school kids what it means to be a team. There are no prima donnas. Everyone is on the same level.

KEITH JACKSON

It's a different time, we're working under a different set of rules in some instances, but I know we believe in some of the same things as earlier Packer championship teams. I know we do. Commitment, discipline, great work ethic. Those are things I try to instill in my team. High-character people working very hard for a common goal.

MIKE HOLMGREN

Desmond Howard. Green Bay, 1997.

Well, we feel like we're the best secret in the league. The invisible receivers. We don't mind that. I'm happy here. Maybe my critics aren't happy, but I'm happy, my coaches are happy, my wife is happy, my kids are happy. Everybody loves it.

ANDRE RISON

We have playmakers on our team and you saw the playmakers make plays. You saw Rison. You saw Freeman. You saw Howard. You saw Reggie White. You saw a host of players.

ANTONIO FREEMAN

I take my hat off to my teammates for not only making me a better receiver, but a better person.

ANDRE RISON

Me and Andre go way back, and believe me, this is the best place for both of us. This can be a tough place to come into, but Andre knows he's well-loved.

BRETT FAVRE

I sure do like the way it feels. The tradition of Green Bay. The fans. Lambeau Field. Vince Lombardi. You can't do nothing but have Packermania. It's funny, I'm a part of it. People really can't believe it, but I'm a Cheesehead.

ANDRE RISON

Edgar Bennett. Green Bay, 1997.

I always envision myself scoring. That makes it much easier in a game. Then it's *deja vu*, it's like I've been there before. But I never, ever imagined myself winning the MVP.

DESMOND HOWARD

I was joking with Desmond before the game. I was like, "Don't take every kick back, let the offensive get a couple of reps in."

DORSEY LEVENS

Our special teams have gotten better and better all year. And they know that if they make the right block and do the right thing, if they get the job done, then Desmond can score every single time he gets the ball.

MIKE HOLMGREN

I was just another strong link in this very, very strong chain.

DESMOND HOWARD

That's what Desmond Howard has done all year for us. Whenever we've struggled or staggered, he's been there. He's been the guy that's lifted this football team up.

ANTONIO FREEMAN

Think about that, six kicks returned for touchdowns. That's phenomenal.

DON BEEBE

Desmond is an unbelievable player. We love watching him play.

BRETT FAVRE

Brett is basically my MVP.

DESMOND HOWARD

Brett Favre. Green Bay, 1997.

God sent me here. Four years ago a lot of people said I was crazy. But now I'm getting a ring. How crazy am I now?

REGGIE WHITE

Week in and week out, people continued to doubt our character. The writers, they are not bad writers, but they don't know what makes a football team come together. They don't know a team's heart. We may not be flashy or sexy or flamboyant, but we won this one.

SEAN JONES

God always has the last laugh.

REGGIE WHITE

It's a little overwhelming. But I can tell you this: it is really gratifying to win this game, really gratifying.

SEAN JONES

This is why we all came to Green Bay.

BRETT FAVRE

It's hard to find any negatives in a positive place.

ANDRE RISON

I'm proud of our football team. I'm pleased how they handled these two weeks of preparation. We have a team of very high-character people. I think that helps you win games. I know it does.

MIKE HOLMGREN

Brett Favre. Green Bay, 1997.

Every guy in the world would like to win a Super Bowl. There's nothing better. To have accomplished this at such a young age is the greatest feeling in the world.

BRETT FAVRE

When you win the big one in high school, there is always a bigger one to win. When you win the big one in college, there is always something bigger to win. There is nothing bigger than this.

AARON TAYLOR

There's nothing else like this in sports. This is better than winning a gold medal in the Olympics. This is better than the World Series.

DON BEEBE

It's hard to put into words the feelings you have after an experience like this. I'm so proud of the football team and the way they handled this week and the whole season.

MIKE HOLMGREN

I made a decision to come here for a reason. I thought this team had a chance to win the Super Bowl. I thought we had a quarterback who could lead us and a coach who could build us. Everything has come to pass.

REGGIE WHITE

To win this, it's unbelievable. We waited a long time for this.

BRETT FAVRE

Our guys work together so good. This week was just a testament of us hanging together and caring about one another, and of us working together for seven months.

REGGIE WHITE

Right now, I'm at the top of the world, and I'm feeling very, very good about it.

MIKE HOLMGREN

Green Bay, 1997.

Honors are great, but what I'm after is the Super Bowl. If I don't win that, everything else will go by the way-side.

BRETT FAVRE

When you get a chance to get a quarterback that you think has a chance to be a great one, you do it. You look for something special, and I thought Brett was gifted physically and had a great arm. He had the tools, but it was up to him. Could he discipline himself? Could he become an artist, a passer, and not just a thrower? I think he has.

MIKE HOLMGREN

When we got the opportunities to make plays, we made 'em. You need a little luck along the way to win a game like this, but we've got a great offense, we've got the best defense in football, and we've got the best return man, probably ever. We've believed in ourselves from the start, but there's a difference in believing it and doing it.

BRETT FAVRE

So much is made in the media about Brett's slow starts. But in the biggest game of his life, he was huge. He threw the ball right where it had to be, and we were able to make some big catches. I'm not surprised at all.

ANTONIO FREEMAN

That's what I do best, move around. I like it when I'm out of the pocket. I can find guys.

BRETT FAVRE

You can't say enough about Brett Favre. You talk about a guy who was vindicated? All the stuff he has gone through this year. The guy is the hardest worker, he never lost his focus, and he's the most easy-going guy around.

SEAN JONES

I'd like to know how many people bet against me this season because they all lost.

BRETT FAVRE

Green Bay, 1997.

This trophy was named after Vince Lombardi. As important as it is to every player in the league, it's more important to us. This is where it belongs. To the coaches, players, organization, trainers, equipment people, this trophy is for every one in the Green Bay Packer organization.

MIKE HOLMGREN

When we land that plane, we drive around that town and see all those crazy fans and then get in that stadium with 60,000 screaming fans and they will not shut up, I tell you, to win a Super Bowl in Green Bay is the ulitmate for any player.

DON BEEBE

We said all year we were winning the championship for the state of Wisconsin and the city of Green Bay. It's the greatest place in the world, and I'm sure it's going to be a state holiday. It will be a ticker tape parade, and they'll only be able to throw it off of a three story building, but that's okay.

SEAN JONES

We get to take a lot of pride back to Green Bay. That's the main thing. The trophy is named after Mr. Lombardi. It's nice to take it back to his home. It's like we reinstate the legacy. It's the sweetest feeling in the world. It's like bringing a family heirloom back that's been gone for so many years.

WILLIAM HENDERSON

Now it is not just Packer fever. It is like a frenzy. The fans took it to another level.

BOB KUBERSKI

I think it's pretty crazy, really. I don't know where they came up with those Cheeseheads, but that's one thing about the people of Wisconsin, they love their football, and they'll do anything to support us.

BRETT FAVRE

We got the best fans right here. They're not afraid to show us, and we're not afraid to tell them.

ADAM TIMMERMAN

Mike Holmgren. Green Bay, 1997.

First of all, I'm really humbled by the experience. This is the greatest group of players that I've ever been around, the most unselfish group of players that I've been around. Coach Lombardi left a wonderful legacy for the rest of us, and now we're trying to do our part to add to it. I hope we can do it for a long time to come. I think what the Lombardi Era has meant to the league and in particular to the Packer organization should never be put to rest.

MIKE HOLMGREN

You see a lot of those guys, the Hornungs, the Willie Woods, you see those guys walking around the facilities. And they want it for us just as bad as we do. That's big time when you get guys from thirty years ago who won the Super Bowl coming back and they're your biggest fans.

ANTONIO FREEMAN

All of those guys are very, very proud of us, and I think they're eager for us to get there. A lot of people say you're taking the glory away from the teams in the past and if your guys win, people will forget about them. That's preposterous. When you have a team like the Green Bay Packers and have that tradition and that pride and that family, then it is just going to add to it. It's not going to take anything away from anyone else.

AARON TAYLOR

One day there'll be some other Packers walking around here, new coach, and people will be saying, "I'm tired of hearing about Brett Favre and Mike Holmgren and Reggie White."

BRETT FAVRE

They're over the top now. They don't have to listen to all the Lombardi stuff anymore. They can bury that, but I know they will bury it with pride.

PAUL HORNUNG